Managing Stress in Schools

Resources in Education

MANAGING STRESS IN SCHOOLS

Marie Brown
and
Sue Ralph
University of Manchester, School of Education

Northcote House

© Copyright 1994 by Marie Brown & Sue Ralph

First published in 1994 by Northcote House Publishers Ltd, Plymbridge House, Estover Road, Plymouth PL6 7PZ, United Kingdom. Tel: Plymouth (0752) 735251. Fax: (0752) 695699. Telex: 45635.

British Library Cataloguing-in-Publication Date.
A catalogue record for this book is available from the British Library.

ISBN 0-7463-0652-0
Typeset by PDQ Typesetting, Stoke-on-Trent
Printed and bound by BPC Wheatons Ltd, Exeter

Contents

Introduction

Stress is an increasing problem faced by teachers in schools. Most of the major teaching unions during the last ten to fifteen years have conducted research into teacher stress. In *Managing Stress: Guidelines for Teachers* (1990, p2) the Assistant Masters and Mistresses Association (AMMA) points out that:

> 'Few would now dispute that teaching is a stressful profession, and it is widely acknowledged that the National Curriculum, LMS and other Educational Reform Act developments are exacerbating an already tense situation.'

These surveys have highlighted the most common sources of stress in classrooms and schools. The most frequently cited stressors include:

- the introduction of the National Curriculum, GCSE, assessment and testing without adequate resourcing;
- violence and poor discipline in the classroom;
- badly designed buildings;
- reorganisation of schools;
- pressure from parents;
- heavy workloads;
- change factors, especially the rate of change without consultation; and
- poor management and organisation in schools.

The surveys found that excessive stress resulted in a number of physical symptoms and psychological problems in teachers. These included:

- higher than average drinking and smoking;
- low resistance to fatigue and infection;
- a high rate of absenteeism amongst teachers;
- an increased incidence of heart disease.

There is no doubt that too much stress is bad for people. Since stress in teachers is increasing, managing stress is crucial if we are to have healthy schools and consequently healthy teachers and pupils.

This book is the result of many years of teaching about stress management and of research into its causes, symptoms and management. It was written to provide practical help for individual teachers, groups of teachers and whole school staffs. The authors have had considerable experience in working with groups of teachers and helping them to identify the things which cause them stress. They have enabled teachers to develop strategies to assist both schools and individuals to manage stress levels. The material is the result of many in-service courses and lectures, and the exercises, activities and suggestions it contains are well tried and tested. We have attempted to make this a practical book which can be used by most teachers and school staffs.

There is still a stigma attached to the idea that teachers are suffering from stress, and they are often reluctant to discuss the problem in case it may indicate to colleagues and superiors that they are in some way failing and not up to the job. We would like to emphasise that for a teacher to admit to feeling stressed is a sign of great strength and is a positive attitude to take. There is considerable evidence to suggest that excessive stress, maintained for long periods of time, can be extremely damaging to one's health, family, job, relationships and to oneself. Although this book concentrates on stress at work, particularly in teaching, it must be emphasised that stress cannot be looked at in isolation but should be considered in the context of the whole person. Individual teachers need to recognise, or be helped to recognise and analyse for themselves, signs and causes of stress especially in the work area. They then need to decide on appropriate management strategies for its resolution. Headteachers and senior managers need to recognise that the acknowledgement of stress is *not* a sign of laziness, incompetence or weakness and they need to reassure individual teachers that they will not lose professional esteem by admitting to it.

A 'whole school' approach to the management of stress is therefore something which policy makers in schools need to consider carefully. Stress in teaching is inherent in the way many teachers are expected to work, both in primary and secondary schools today. We feel that only an organisational approach can provide the appropriate help for school teachers under extreme pressure. It is important for school management to ensure that the process begins with a 'whole school' debate and that all staff are involved in the planning and implementation of strategies agreed, ie 'whole school' stress reduction policies and plans. Some plans may be easily and quickly implemented, whereas others may involve quite a radical restructuring of existing processes and procedures. We would encourage school management to formulate stress action plans as we are strongly of the opinion that managing stress is a whole school issue which may well require a modification of culture and attitudes in many schools.

Marie Brown
Sue Ralph

1

What is Stress?

There is a growing realisation that stress for teachers is an increasing problem. Stress as a likely cause of illness, problems and personal misery is giving rise to growing public as well as medical and scientific concern. Hardly a day goes by without there being some reference to the phenomenon in the popular media and magazines abound with 'questionnaires' for us to measure our levels of stress. This media interest is both a good and a bad thing. It is good in the sense that it brings the issues to a wider audience but bad in the sense that it can trivialise what is a very serious subject. Most teachers have an increased awareness of the effects of stress. Teachers and their organisations would agree that the effects of long-term stress in particular are very severe.

Stress in teachers has been the subject of much research since the 1930s and has been described recently as the teachers' number one health problem (Stuart Nattrass in *Teacher's Weekly*, 31 January 1991).

There are many definitions of stress and we will consider a few of them. Ellison (1990) defines it as a biochemical response by the body to a threatening situation (*stressor*). Although this response is meant to ensure self-survival, the frequent changes in blood pressure caused by regular exposure to stressors can lead to severe illness, including heart disease, in the future. Stress is specific to each individual. What one teacher might find stressful is not necessarily stressful for another. In addition, several teachers in the same stressful situation will probably respond very differently. This non-specificity of the nature of stress makes it difficult to produce a simple cause and effect model (AMMA 1987b).

Stress, depending on how it is experienced, can be negative or positive. Teachers can find it stimulating and challenging in which case stress is positive, or it can be the cause of varying states of anxiety and depression: here it can be harmful. Too much stress causes physiological and psychological problems for individuals. Although Selye (1956) described stress in a positive manner (see Activity Three, page 18) the term stress in common usage is usually

11

found at the negative end of the spectrum.

'The word stress is used in the sense of "distress" which people experience from too many or too few pressures and strains. Distress is something which occurs to all of us, as does happiness. It is only when there is too much distress, physical or mental, that problems start.'

(Bailey, D. 1987 Part 4 p4)

Hans Selye produced a model which had four dimensions to it:

1. **Overstress**: where we have too high a workload and the demands of the job are greater than the individual teachers are likely to manage.
2. **Understress**: where we have too little work to do and this leads to understimulation, boredom and possibly lack of motivation and depression.
3. **Good stress**: when we find something really challenging and motivating.
4. **Bad stress**: that which makes us feel exhausted and irritable and frustrated.

Tom Cox described stress at work as:

'... to do with coping, or failing to cope with the demands and constraints placed on the person. It is to do with the person's realisation that they have a problem which they cannot adequately or easily deal with.'

(1987, p1)

Some studies have suggested a relationship between personality and stress. For example the work of Friedman and Rosenman (1974) suggested that certain personality factors were related to higher levels of stress. They identified **Type A** personalities (workaholics, restless and aggressive) as being more prone to coronary disease than their peers whilst **Type B** (calm and relaxed) appear to be slower and steadier. However other findings suggest that it is not possible to say that particular traits will definitely lead to stress, simply that it is more likely that there may be a vicious cycle of interaction between stress and certain personality traits, with one tending to reinforce the other (Rees 1989).

For the purpose of this book we are going to regard a stressful issue as being one which you feel that you cannot cope with successfully and which causes you to experience unwanted physical, emotional or mental reactions.

Stress will become a problem if there is a discrepancy between the demands on a teacher and his/her ability to manage. It therefore follows that the amount of stress which a person can withstand is differentiated according to the individual (Ellison, 1990).

ORGANISATIONAL STRESS

It is important to consider the wider question of the stress that may be inherently present in an organisation. We must consider both the individual and the organisation in which he/she works. All forms of organisation are potential causes of stress. The AMMA (1987b) Report was especially concerned that stress should be reduced and 'positively transformed' and suggested that organisational stress management and individual stress handling strategies should be employed in schools. If the organisation creates an imbalance by inappropriate demands on staff in terms of the mismatch between the work loads of teachers and the abilities of individual teachers to meet them, stress reduction strategies must be implemented. On individual stress handling the report recommends that if teachers are given the skills necessary to manage their stress, both the individual and the organisation will benefit. An organisation that has a large number of highly stressed teachers will not be good for, or effective in, any organisational capacity.

CAUSES OF STRESS IN TEACHERS

The causes of stress may be different for each individual teacher or group of teachers, but certain work related factors emerge as common throughout:

Relationships with pupils
- changes in pupil attitude and motivation;
- anxiety over test and examination results;
- perceived lack of discipline;
- over-large class size;
- mixed ability classes.

Relationships with colleagues
- poor lines of communication at all levels;
- lack of community spirit;
- personality clashes;
- lack of academic and social intercourse between departments;
- workloads unevenly distributed.

Relationships with parents and the wider community
- pressure from parents to achieve good results;
- perceived impending threat of 'payment by results';
- dealing with unrealistic expectations;
- increased parental involvement and access which can lead to possible conflicts;
- general societal cynicism about the role of teachers;
- poor pay and status;
- media bashing.

Innovation and change
- constant demands for change for no good reason;
- feelings of powerlessness and failure;
- rate of change;
- lack of information and resources to support and facilitate change.

School management and administration
- poor overall school organisation;
- little real involvement in decision making;
- poor communication models;
- lack of staff development to meet new demands of job;
- lack of support from school administration in the face of increasing paperwork;
- inadequate staff facilities, storage areas and personal work spaces;
- poor technical backup.

Time factors
- increasing number and variety of tasks;
- increasing number of educational demands outside of school time which could lead to conflict with family and friends;
- frequency and poor organisation of formal and informal meetings.

Not all of the above stressors may apply to all teachers. Some of them may be viewed as positive challenges. What is important, however, is that teachers identify, or are helped to identify, factors which are stressful to them. They should be encouraged to take the necessary steps to manage stress at a personal level and thus open up the debate whereby school staffs, governing bodies and local education authorities will be encouraged to take the matter seriously and begin to identify ways in which teachers can be supported.

STRESS IS GOOD FOR US

Some stress is good for us. We all need a certain amount of stress in order to perform well. Problems occur when there is too much or too little stress. This can be best illustrated by looking at the graph below which describes the relationship between the amount of stress experienced by an individual and his/her performance and health and well-being. Work overload is compounded by irregular hours, stimulants (caffeine) and neglect of the home, leisure, and the family.

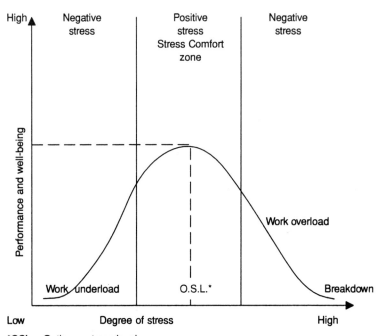

*OSL – Optimum stress level

Job performance
Adapted from Margaret Parkinson, (1985) Training the Counsellors – 2. *Stress Management in Education and Training*, September 1985, page 226.

As we can see, when our degree of stress is very low or very high our performance levels and general well-being are low. As our stress levels increase so does our performance and well-being until we reach our *stress comfort zone*. Within this zone we all have an optimum stress level which varies from individual to individual and from activity to activity and is the point at which we function most effectively. We all need to be able to recognise this point in ourselves

15

and to employ stress management strategies to keep ourselves within this area. The point of optimum stress level, the peak within our stress comfort zone, is where we function most effectively. We feel good, have a high level of self confidence and are alert. At either side of this optimum point we can deal with extra levels of stress fairly easily (either in the areas of understimulation or overstimulation) but as we go further away from the point of optimum stress level, the effect can become increasingly serious. For example, as we move further along the curve and into the negative area of too much stress, we first of all experience:

- Tiredness
- Fatigue
- Ill health
- Burnout
- Serious ill health
- Breakdown
- Death

In order to help teachers and their managers recognise their stress comfort zones, Parkinson identified the following five categories as signs of stress teachers should be aware of when operating outside their stress comfort zones:

Physiological
These might include headaches, lots of different aches and pains, sweating, panting, not being able to sleep, changes in blood pressure, increased heart beat, frequent minor illnesses, dry throat and mouth, indigestion and so on.

Cognitive
These might include mind blanks, a general loss of interest in work, low levels of concentration, periods of forgetfulness etc.

Emotional
These might include anxiety, crying for no apparent reason, depression, irritability, feeling nervous, withdrawal and so on.

Behavioural
These might include increased dependency on prescribed drugs,

increased smoking and drinking, changes in eating habits, grinding of teeth, nervous tics, high-pitched nervous inappropriate laughter, being impulsive, trembling etc.

Spiritual
These might include feelings of hopelessness, questioning tasks, asking what's it all about, what's the point?

Some of the signs of stress are listed in Chapter Two.

The main points to consider
1. There are many definitions of stress.
2. It is perfectly all right to feel stressed. It is normal to admit to feeling stressed.
3. When there is too much or too little stress is the time when the problems occur.
4. Stress is an individual thing. What causes you stress might not cause me stress. It is our personal perception of what causes us to feel stressed that is important. Stress can be caused by almost anything.
5. We really need to look at the 'whole person' and what causes stress in all aspects of that person's life. In this book we are only considering stress at work.

A PLAN FOR MANAGING STRESS

The following represents a plan for managing stress. These ideas will be developed in much greater detail in subsequent chapters. In order to manage our stress we need to follow these steps:

1. Identify the things which cause us stress.
2. Work out a personal stress profile, listing all the items we have identified.
3. Prioritise our list.
4. Work out an action plan.
5. Develop strategies to manage our stress.

The alternative is an unpleasant one, as we will suffer the consequences of not managing our stress, which, as can be seen from the graph, can be severe.

Guidance on how teachers can identify stress is given in Chapter Two. For the purposes of this book we have defined stress as the demands on an individual and the individual's ability to meet those demands. It is the tension in the relationship between the two which is important.

ACTIVITY ONE

What do you understand by the word stress? Write down a few sentences which describe your understanding of this.

_____

_____

_____

If possible discuss what you have written with a partner. Check to see whether you have found any differences or similarities.

ACTIVITY TWO

Do you think that you are suffering from stress? Make a list of any symptoms that you are experiencing.

1._____ 2._____

3._____ 4._____

5._____ 6._____

7._____ 8._____

9._____ 10._____

ACTIVITY THREE

Go back to Activity One. Divide what you have written into negative and positive stress.
Negative stress

_____

_____

_____

Positive stress

_____

_____

_____

Which is the longer list? Can you think of some more examples of positive stress?

ACTIVITY FOUR

Selye (1956) described four types of stress, *Overstress*, *Understress*, *Good stress* and *Bad stress* which he represented on a diagram similar to the one given below. Categorise your stress in terms of the four dimensions.

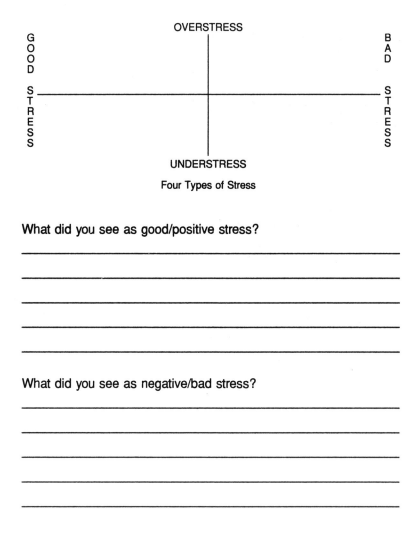

Four Types of Stress

What did you see as good/positive stress?

_____

_____

_____

_____

_____

What did you see as negative/bad stress?

_____

_____

_____

_____

_____

What did you see as Understress/too little stress?

_____

_____

_____

_____

_____

What did you see as Overstress/too much stress?

_____

_____

_____

_____

_____

What can you conclude about your stress pattern?

_____

_____

_____

_____

_____

Discuss this with a partner and decide with him/her where you lie on the stress graph illustrated on page 19. Remember that your objective would be to gain a balance between the Overstress and Understress and to counteract as much of the Bad stress as possible with Good stress.

(This activity and graph have been adapted from Cook, R. (1992) *The Prevention and Management of Stress,* London, pp 5 and 53).

2

Identification of Stress (1): The Individual

'Individuals differ in how they respond to stress; in particular, people interpret and evaluate stressful situations in different ways depending, for instance, on their past experience, personality, beliefs, vulnerabilities and resources. A situation perceived as threatening by one person may be seen as challenging, or of no significance by another.'

(Education Service Advisory Committee, 1990, p21)

As we discussed in Chapter 1, a certain level of stress is necessary for our well-being. Without some stress we cannot function properly as individuals. What is important is that it does not get out of hand. Teachers need to be able to recognise situations in which they experience stress and to take steps to manage this. To do this you will need to be able to:

- know *when* you are experiencing stress;
- know *why* you are experiencing stress;
- think about *how* you might manage it.

RECOGNISING STRESS

Early identification of stress is very important, therefore it is essential for the individual teacher to recognise and analyse for him/herself the signs as soon as they become apparent, as individuals respond to stress in different ways. (Brown, M. and Ralph, S. 1992). Some of the most common signs of stress are listed below. You could use this list to determine whether you are experiencing stress now or might do in the future.

Performance at work
- Frequently feeling like staying off work;
- Inability to manage time well;

- Inability to meet deadlines;
- Inability to concentrate;
- Having a heavy workload;
- Inability to delegate;
- Feelings of inadequacy related to performance at work;
- Job dissatisfaction;
- Taking work home more frequently;
- Low level of productivity.

Relationships with colleagues
- Increased feelings of irritation or aggression;
- Becoming increasingly introverted;
- Inability to relate to colleagues;
- Unwillingness to cooperate;
- Inability to listen to advice or criticism;
- Frequent irrational conflicts at work;
- Cynical, inappropriate humour;
- Demotivation;
- Withdrawing from supportive relationships;
- Lying;
- Role ambiguity;
- Role conflict.

Behavioural and emotional indicators
- Loss of appetite;
- Reduced self-esteem;
- Increased use of alcohol, tranquillisers, coffee, cigarettes etc.;
- Insomnia, bad dreams or nightmares;
- Being unduly fussy;
- Feelings of alienation;
- Loss of confidence;
- Too busy to relax;
- Frequent colds, 'flu or other infections;
- Vague aches or pains;
- Accident prone;
- Persistent negative thoughts;
- Palpitations.

Some of the above signs may not necessarily be stress related but if you find that some of these symptoms apply to you, you may wish to consider stress as the cause. Remember that the same amount of stress can show itself in different ways in different people: some individuals may show just one or two signs while others may manifest several. Responses to stress can vary, both between individuals and over time; some people may primarily experience physical symptoms while others may experience psychological disturbance (Education Services Advisory Committee 1990, p5). A teacher under stress may well induce stress in students and among other colleagues. Teachers under stress may exhibit changes in behaviour which may seriously affect and disrupt the learning of children in individual classrooms. On a larger scale, if several teachers in any one school have high levels of stress, the entire school could be affected in a potentially negative manner.

STRESS PRONE PERSONALITY FACTORS

Meyer Friedman and Ray Rosenman in their book *Type 'A' Behaviour and Your Heart* (Greenwich Publications, 1975), identified two principal types of behaviour patterns; Type 'A' and Type 'B'. They found that coronary patients whom they had studied exhibited similar behaviour patterns. Type 'A' behaviours were the high-risk ones.

Type 'A' Behaviour Characteristics
- Extremely busy;
- Very ambitious;
- Emphasising key words in ordinary speech in an explosive manner;
- A preoccupation with deadlines and getting things done quickly;
- Preoccupation with competition;
- Self-confidence;
- Aggression, hostility and impatience;
- Moving, walking and eating rapidly;
- Guilty about relaxing.

A number of research studies have looked at people who exhibit the characteristics of Type 'A' behaviour in different situations. The following is a summary of the major findings of these studies. These people were more inclined to:

- Pack more things into a shorter space of time;
- Work longer hours;
- Spend more time on school-related work (teachers);
- Sleep for fewer hours;
- Spend less time in relaxational and recreational activities;
- Communicate less with close relations, friends etc.;

- Experience more breakdowns in relationships;
- Have little desire to socialise.

Type 'B' Behaviour Characteristics

Unlike Type 'A' people, Type 'B' people adopt a more realistic view of work and life and are not inclined to take on more than they can cope with. They do not always like to work to deadlines and are better at delegating to those who work for them. They are secure in themselves and in what they do and always maintain a sense of balance in their lives. In most respects their behaviour is almost a mirror image of that of Type 'A'.

Are you Type 'A' or Type 'B'

The above information should help you to identify whether you are a Type 'A' or Type 'B' person. It is important to remember that behaviour in these categories can only be seen as an indicator, as most people lie somewhere between the two extremes. Friedman and Rosenman's work gives some indication of the reasons for the greater incidence of stress-related disease in Type 'A' people. Ways of managing this behaviour will be discussed in a later chapter.

Identifying the causes

If you appear to be manifesting signs of stress, you next need to consider what might be responsible. In some cases the cause may be obvious to you, but in others you may have to spend time in an honest self-examination and/or work with other people to discover it. The crucial thing is to identify your individual stressors and take steps to deal with them. You might find it useful to work with a colleague and brainstorm the things or situations that make you feel under stress. (Activity One). The *Personal Stress Audit* provided in this chapter, along with the stress log diary and personal agenda for action, will help you to start this process.

The following two case studies illustrate the importance of recognition of stress signs while they are at manageable levels and also the importance of the head teachers or other support dimension.

Case Study A

Ms B. aged 45 and divorced, is a history teacher in an urban comprehensive school. She is very conscientious and well-liked by both pupils and staff. She felt herself being increasingly overwhelmed by the demands of the National Curriculum and the rapid rate of change in the education service. She noticed that her intake of alcohol was on the increase and began to experience loss of confidence and self-esteem and this led to further feelings of depression and demotivation. She felt sufficiently concerned to seek professional help and in a series of counselling interviews was encouraged to draw up a personal stress profile and develop ways of managing her stress levels.

Case Study B
Mr G aged 32 and married, is a year three teacher in a suburban primary school. He is a generally competent and capable teacher. He began to experience feelings of increased irritability and aggression towards his colleagues. He frequently came into open conflict with the head teacher and this was having a very disruptive effect on the class which he taught. He became very unpopular in the staff room due to his cynical and caustic comments on education in general and on the school in particular. At this point the head teacher intervened sensibly and effectively by encouraging Mr G to attend a stress management course run by the Local Authority educational psychologist. This course helped him to identify his own stressors and to work out an action plan.

Stress diary
A systematic approach to recognition and identification of stressors is necessary if one is to begin to deal with stress before it assumes unmanageable proportions. A useful technique is to keep a stress diary in which you can 'assess those incidents and series of related incidents during the working days, weeks and months that cause you distress', (Cooper, C. 1988, p167). This diary can provide you with information about the types of situation and people who cause you the most stress. As you become aware of these you can develop an action plan that can help you to manage these situations or eliminate them. '. . . .at the very least it will alert you to when a stressful event (in your terms) is about to take place.' (ibid). At the end of each day you should list all the events and incidents with people that caused you stress. You then should consider:

- what action you took;
- how you felt;
- whether in retrospect you took the correct action?

Other ways of recognising stress and identifying stressors can be through the use of a stress audit, a guided fantasy, and/or a personal stress profile.

Personal stress audit
It is possible to audit individual stress levels by means of a questionnaire. There are many examples of questionnaires designed to measure stress in teachers, but questionnaires are notoriously

difficult to design and their reliability and validity is questionable. We feel that the example given in Activity Three offers a series of questions which could be better used as triggers to help teachers think in a structured way about the things that cause them stress at work.

Guided fantasy
In this technique teachers are asked to choose an incident which would cause them stress. The intention is that they should be encouraged to express their feelings, to realise how strong these can be and to recognise for themselves that stress needs to be worked through their systems. In the fantasy, teachers often choose an actual incident which is past. This is an indication that the incident is still alive for them and has not been worked through successfully. It is useful to have an experienced facilitator to guide participants through. The fantasy schedule is included in the activities (Activity Four).

Personal stress profile
From the results of brainstorming, the personal audit, stress diary and guided fantasy or some of these activities, it should be possible for the teacher to draw up a personal stress profile and agenda for action. The profile can be compiled by grouping sets of stressors under a number of common headings, eg job related, person related, environment related, health related and so on. The stressors could then be listed in order of priority. The individual should now have a very clear picture of what causes him or her stress and should be in a position to begin to think constructively about management strategies.

ACTIVITY ONE

Either on your own or preferably with a colleague, list all the things which cause you stress at work.

1._____ 2._____

3._____ 4._____

5._____ 6._____

7._____ 8._____

9._____ 10._____

Now place each of the above items in order of importance for you. Give each item a score of between one and ten (ten being the most important).

ACTIVITY TWO

Personal Agenda for Action – Part Two
Consider the list that you made in Activity One. Write down your stressors in order of importance for you and indicate by the side of each one if you consider that this could be dealt with at an individual or organisational level.

STRESSOR	INDIVIDUAL LEVEL	ORGANISATIONAL LEVEL
1.		
2.		
3.		
4.		
5.		
6.		
7.		
8.		
9.		
10.		

ACTIVITY THREE

Completing a personal stress audit
Listed below are some factors which it is thought could create tension or stress at work. Look at the questions and for each situation place a tick in the appropriate column (ie if it creates tension and how often this happens). Please add to the list. Its purpose is to help you identify situations which cause you stress.

Stress Questions Section One
The following are situations which might cause you to feel stressed. Look at each of the situations and place a tick in the appropriate column.

| | CREATES SERIOUS STRESS | CREATES MILD STRESS | CREATES NO STRESS |
| SITUATION | | | |

1. Working on your own_____
2. Being criticised_____
3. Being appraised_____
4. Having to meet new people eg parents, officials etc_____
5. Having to speak in public_____
6. Having to speak at meetings_____
7. Having no responsibility_____
8. Working to a deadline_____
9. Not having clear priorities_____
10. Having a large workload_____
11. Facing change_____
12. Feeling powerless_____
13. Being ignored_____
14. Travelling a long distance_____
15. Having to deal with the feelings of other people_____
16. Arriving late_____
17. Job uncertainty_____
18. Short-term contracts_____
19. Dealing with anger/conflict_____
20. Expressing feelings_____
21. Contact with senior management_____
22. Dealing with problems of discipline_____
23. Dealing with loss of status_____
24. Increasing administrative tasks_____

(*Insert your own situations*)

25. _____
26. _____
27. _____
28. _____

Stress Questions Section Two

Listed below are some common problems identified by teachers as causing them stress. Indicate by circling the appropriate number to what extent they are a problem for you.

ROLE AMBIGUITY

	Definitely No			Definitely Yes	
I am clear what my responsibilities are	1	2	3	4	5
I am clear what is expected of me	1	2	3	4	5
I allocate my time well	1	2	3	4	5
I have a clear job specification	1	2	3	4	5
I know the extent of my authority	1	2	3	4	5
Clearly planned goals and objectives exist for my job	1	2	3	4	5
I have clear guidelines for my work	1	2	3	4	5

Stress Questions Section Three

Teachers often have many different roles in schools. How comfortable do you feel in these roles?

MULTIPLE ROLES

ROLE	Very Comfortable			Very Uncomfortable	
Teacher	1	2	3	4	5
Counsellor	1	2	3	4	5
Tutor	1	2	3	4	5
Curriculum Developer	1	2	3	4	5
Public Speaker	1	2	3	4	5
Marketing Expert	1	2	3	4	5
Administrator	1	2	3	4	5
Committee Member	1	2	3	4	5
Committee Chair/Secretary	1	2	3	4	5
Course coordinator	1	2	3	4	5
Examiner	1	2	3	4	5
Assessor	1	2	3	4	5
Liaison Person	1	2	3	4	5
Referral Person	1	2	3	4	5
Financial Expert	1	2	3	4	5
Staff Developer	1	2	3	4	5
Change Agent	1	2	3	4	5
Disciplinarian	1	2	3	4	5
Others	1	2	3	4	5

Stress Questions Section Four

ROLE CONFLICT

I feel role conflict when:

	Definitely No			Definitely Yes
I am asked to do things which I feel should be done very differently	1	2	3	4	5
I am responsible to several different people who have quite different ideas about how the work should be done	1	2	3	4	5
I frequently do things which are acceptable to one person but not to others	1	2	3	4	5
I receive incompatible requests from two or more people	1	2	3	4	5
I feel that I do not receive support from the people I work with	1	2	3	4	5
I often work on unnecessary things	1	2	3	4	5
I am often asked to do things in a hurry	1	2	3	4	5
I receive work to do without the necessary resources to carry this out	1	2	3	4	5
I have work to do without adequate resources to back it up	1	2	3	4	5
I find it difficult to get the information that I need	1	2	3	4	5

Stress Questions Section Five
Teaching involves increasing responsibilities for both people and 'things'. Role overload is having too many responsibilities and role underload is having too few responsibilities.

ROLE OVERLOAD/UNDERLOAD

Responsibility for 'things'

How do you feel about the following	Very Comfortable				Very Uncomfortable
Responsibility for initiating and implementing course work?	1	2	3	4	5
Responsibility for keeping adequate records?	1	2	3	4	5
Responsibility for equipment and facilities?	1	2	3	4	5
Responsibility for budgets and expenditure?	1	2	3	4	5
Responsibility for maintaining and ensuring standards?	1	2	3	4	5

Responsibility for 'People'

Responsibility for teaching staff?	1	2	3	4	5
Responsibility for technical staff?	1	2	3	4	5
Responsibility for secretarial staff?	1	2	3	4	5
Responsibility for ancillary staff?	1	2	3	4	5
Responsibility for the future of others?	1	2	3	4	5
Responsibility for the future careers of others?	1	2	3	4	5
Responsibility for the timetables of other staff?	1	2	3	4	5
Responsibility for ensuring that others work adequately?	1	2	3	4	5
Responsibility for part-time members of staff?	1	2	3	4	5

ACTIVITY FOUR: GUIDED FANTASY

For this activity you need to work in pairs, with a facilitator. You will need to think of a time when you felt very stressed and make some notes about this under the three headings given: Thinking, Feeling, Doing. We have given an example of an incident that we find stressful, '*Waiting to be interviewed*'. Under the three headings, we have started to explore what we might be *thinking*, ie 'I'll be glad when this is over'; what we might be *feeling*, ie frightened and apprehensive; and how we might be *behaving*, ie going to the loo, walking or pacing up and down etc.

What happens to me when I'm stressed?

WAITING TO BE INTERVIEWED

Thinking	*Feeling*	*Behaviour/doing*
I'll be glad when this is over.	Frightened/ Apprehensive.	Going to the loo; Walking about; Sweating palms; Fidgeting.

In order to help you think more deeply about this, the facilitator can guide you through a series of questions which might help you to remember your thoughts, feelings and behaviour.

It is important that participants are reassured that they will not be asked to discuss the actual incident (*unless they wish to do so*). They will be asked to discuss in pairs how they felt, what their thoughts were and how they behaved and to make some general points to the whole group.

1. Remember an incident which made you feel very stressed.

2. Sit comfortably, close your eyes and let yourself go back to that situation.

3. Remember as much detail as you can.

4. How old were you at this time?

5. Where were you at this time? Were you in a room, an open space? Think of your environment at this time.

6. Were you alone? Who else was there? What were you wearing? What were the other people wearing?
7. What were your feelings at that time?
8. Go into your body; what are your feelings now? Where are you experiencing these feelings?
9. What did you do after this incident?
10. What did you tell yourself after this incident?
11. Have you been in that situation again/before?
12. What did you really want to do in that situation? What stopped you?
13. What did you learn from that situation?
14. When was the incident over for you? Is it really over?
15. What positive things can you learn from this example?

This activity will take about 30 minutes to complete. It should be used as part of a total stress reduction programme and the facilitator should debrief the exercise, using it to illustrate to participants that stress can leave strong feelings, which need to be managed, and that excessive stress can be harmful. The debrief, usually whole group based, normally takes an additional 20 minutes.

3

Identification of Stress (2): The School

It is not sufficient just for individual teachers to identify and devise management strategies for themselves; the whole organisation of the school needs to recognise the symptoms of stress in itself and provide an impetus for its identification. We therefore recommend that a whole school approach to stress management should be adopted. Senior managers have an obligation to their staffs to help them identify and manage their stress. Too many highly stressed members of any school staff can seriously affect the performance of any school.

HOW SCHOOLS CAN IDENTIFY STRESS

This will involve senior management identifying the sources of stress in their own schools. It is very important that this is done so that plans can be drawn up to alleviate the situation as soon as possible. It is essential that all staff are fully involved in the identification of school stressors and the drawing up of an action plan to alleviate them.

As we have already indicated elsewhere in this book, stress levels are very much features which are dependent on the individual teacher and the individual school. What is stressful for one teacher in one school is not stressful for another teacher in another school. A useful starting point in the identification of whole school stressors may lie in a consideration of the concepts of organisational climate and health. Schools, like other organisations, have climates which can have very powerful effects on the individuals working in them without their being aware of it. Ideas of climate need to be understood because a poor school climate can often be the cause of stress amongst its teachers. Knowing about the climate of your school can help you as a staff to move towards taking steps to developing a whole school approach to the management of stress.

Anyone who has visited a number of schools will have been struck by their different 'feel'. Some schools actually seem to be reflected in people's bright faces and one suspects that they are optimistic and happy workplaces, whilst in others there is the equally subjective impression that there is a dark, tense and threatening atmosphere with the staff and pupils conveying a melancholy air of resignation. It is reasonable to assume, then, that an open, happy and healthy work environment leads to a less stressed staff. The climate and health of a school, therefore, are important concepts in the identification of school stress.

Openness

Firstly, what is meant by an open climate? Halpin and Croft (1963) identified critical aspects of teacher-teacher and teacher-head teacher interactions in American schools. They constructed the organisational climate descriptive questionnaire (OCDQ) which attempted to map and measure the climates of schools along an open to closed continuum. This questionnaire was redesigned by Hoy et al. 1991 who developed two new and simplified versions of the OCDQ, for primary schools and secondary schools. The four areas of open to closed climate which are thrown up by this questionnaire are as follows:

1. **Supportive head teacher behaviour**: is shown when the head teacher is helpful, genuinely concerned with teachers and attempts to motivate them by using constructive criticism and setting an example through hard work.

2. **Directive head teacher behaviour**: is characterised by rigid and domineering control. The head teacher closely monitors all teachers and school activities down to the smallest detail.

3. **Engaged teacher behaviour**: this reflects a teaching staff in which teachers are proud of their school, enjoy working with each other, are supportive of their colleagues and committed to the success of their students.

4. **Frustrated teacher behaviour**: this describes a teaching staff that feels itself burdened with routine duties, administrative paperwork and excessive assignments unrelated to teaching. It is where the teacher as a person is ignored.

This questionnaire does not explain: it merely describes. It measures how teachers in schools interact with the head teacher and each other. What it *does* do is to reveal the foundations for organisational self-analysis and as such may be a powerful instrument for identification of school stress. Open schools are likely to be schools where the issue of stress is debated at all levels while in closed schools it is not likely to be on the agenda at all.

Now try **Activity One** (page 39). This should ideally be a whole school activity and could usefully form the basis of a whole school staff training day on stress.

School health

Organisational health is another framework for looking at the general atmosphere of a school. It refers to teachers' perceptions of their work environment. A healthy school is protected from unreasonable community and parental pressures. The governors successfully resist all narrow efforts of vested interest groups to influence policy. The head teacher is a dynamic leader, is supportive of teachers, yet provides and expects high standards of performance. The teachers themselves are committed to both teaching and learning. Teachers set high but achievable standards for their pupils and promote a serious and orderly learning environment. Classroom resources are always available. Teachers are proud of their school, which they readily identify with, and have a lot of trust in one another both personally and professionally. Organisational health can be measured by the Organisational Health Inventory (OHI).

The dimensions of organisational health which are measured by the Organisational Health Inventory are as follows:

- **At the institutional level**: Institutional integrity is defined as a school that has integrity in its educational curriculum. The school is not vulnerable to narrow, vested interests of community groups; indeed teachers are protected from unreasonable community and parental demands. The school is able to cope successfully with outside forces.

- **At the managerial level**: Initiating structure. This is where the head teacher makes his/her attitudes clear to the teaching staff and maintains definite standards of performance.

- **Consideration**: This is defined as head teacher behaviour that is friendly, supportive and collegial. The head teacher looks out for the welfare of the staff and is open to their suggestions.

- **Head teacher influence**: This is defined as the head teacher's ability to affect the actions of superiors. The influential head teacher is persuasive, works effectively with superiors yet demonstrates independence in thought and action.

- **Resource support**: This refers to a school where adequate classroom supplies and teaching materials are available and extra materials are easily obtained.

- **At the technical level**: Morale. This is defined as the sense of trust, confidence, enthusiasm and friendliness among teachers. Teachers feel good about each other and, at the same time, feel a sense of accomplishment from their jobs.

- **Academic emphasis**: This refers to the school's drive for achievement. High but achievable goals are set for students; the learning environment is orderly and serious; teachers believe pupils can achieve; and pupils work hard and respect those who do well (Hoy et al. 1991).

Now try **Activity Two** (page 40). Again this should ideally be a whole school activity. Details of the questionnaires and scoring can be found in Hoy et al. (1991).

The questionnaires on climate and health will give us some idea of the staff culture of our schools and may help to describe the complicated interpersonal processes at work in highly stressed school staffs. Reynolds (1987) says that the staff culture of an 'inadequate' school may show many of the characteristics of an 'inadequate' or insecure person. These are:

- projection of individual teachers' deficiencies on to the children or their parents as excuse for ineffectiveness;
- 'cling-ons' of past practice (we've always done it this way);
- defences, whereby teachers have built walls round themselves to keep out threatening messages from outsiders;
- fear of attempting change because it may fail, associated with a reluctance to take risks;
- the fantasy that change is someone else's job;
- the 'safety in numbers' ploy, whereby the staff retreat into a ring-fenced mentality.

Many of the above are defensive mechanisms which are sometimes employed by highly stressed school staffs to protect themselves from outside influences. They have important implications for senior managers in schools as no school leader can afford to neglect the school climate that is most likely to be supportive of staff growth and improvement. It must constantly be assessed, strengthened and, where necessary, altered. The climate must be capable of acknowledging, respecting and valuing teachers. It must at the same time make teachers responsive to the expectations of the wider community and environment. The climate of a school must bind the school in a healthy set of working relationships which are supportive, committed to common goals and continuous improvement. Schools which value, develop and support the judgement and expertise of all their staff are likely to be schools in which teachers will not be unduly stressed.

While school climate and health may be very important factors in the identification of sources of whole school stress they are not the only factors to take into account. Union and other stress reports have revealed the following problems in schools and have highlighted many which they perceive to be important sources of stress.

1. *Lack of resources*: Teachers currently suffer from a lack of resources or perceive that they suffer from a lack of resources largely due to government policies since 1988. This will have important implications for teachers' working environments as they will not do a good job if they feel that they are being deprived of the tools of their trade.

2. *Lack of administrative support*: This seems to be particularly problematic in primary schools where much of the head teacher's time is often taken up with bureaucratic duties. Increased administrative duties for all teachers leads to lack of preparation time and increased workloads.

3. *Poor working environment*: Torrington and Weightman (1989) in *The Reality of School Management* (Blackwell) have highlighted the issue of poor working conditions in schools, particularly the appalling state of some of the staff rooms in some secondary schools and the lack of staff rooms in some primary schools. Teachers need somewhere to relax and switch off as well as the provision of a quiet working area. They also need to be confident that the teaching rooms in which they work and other staff facilities are clean and well maintained.

4. *Teacher workloads*: Due to the demands of the national curriculum and its associated assessment procedures, teachers are now reporting much more intensive workloads than ever before.

5. *School staffing*: Due to budget decisions, some schools may not be as well staffed as they have been previously because of financial constraints and this may add to already stressful situations.

6. *Time constraints*: Administrative duties have also increased since the 1988 Act. This may result in less contact time for teachers due to the increased bureaucratic nature of their jobs. Extra demands are frequently made on teachers which result in them having to work even more at home, and results in even more stress.

7. *Poor management of schools at all levels*: This was also a finding of

the Torrington and Weightman study and is frequently mentioned by teachers as a major dissatisfier.

8. *Poor communication*: Staff frequently perceive a divide between 'them and us' and report feelings of being devalued, ignored and poorly motivated. Poor communication systems in schools are also frequently quoted as a major source of stress.

Now try **Activity One.**

ACTIVITY ONE

You could perhaps do the following activity on a school-based inservice training day. With a group of colleagues make a list of the things which you perceive as stressful in your school organisation and environment. Compare your list with the list in this chapter. You may have many more to add.

1. _____

2. _____

3. _____

4. _____

5. _____

6. _____

7. _____

8. _____

9. _____

10. _____

This could be a departmental or a non departmental activity.

Another way of identifying whole school stress is by the use of OCDQ and OHI questionnaires. These can be given to the whole school staff and the responses collated to give a profile of the particular areas of school work where the organisational health is poor.

ACTIVITY TWO

Fill in the appropriate climate or health questionnaire or both for your school. Full details of the questionnaires and scoring can be found in Hoy et al (1991).

Individual teachers can identify stressors and then develop stress management strategies for themselves. In addition the organisation, ie the school, needs to look carefully at itself and see what can be done to make it a less stressful environment in which to work. Stressful situations may occur because of:

- the organisation's culture;
- function;
- structure;
- the nature of its general and specialist management;
- poor recruitment and/or selection procedures;
- environments not designed for modern courses;
- teachers not trained sufficiently well or recently to meet the changing demands.

HOW SCHOOLS CAN MANAGE STRESS

After identifying areas of stress in their schools, head teachers and senior managers need to involve their staffs in developing stress reduction policies and plans. It is important to remember that stress should be tackled at both the individual and the school level. Senior management should remember that the organisation itself can cause stress. It is essential that an empathetic ethos is developed in the school where stress management is a serious commitment on both sides. A warm and supportive atmosphere is necessary so that teachers are enabled to discuss their concerns. The attitude – that it is a strength to be able to admit that some things cause you to feel stressed – is to be encouraged.

Stress reduction policies and action plans need to be developed. Some of these plans can be quickly and easily implemented; others may involve a radical rethink and restructuring of existing policies and processes. It is, however, crucial that stress management is part of an ongoing debate in schools.

Appraisal

Appraisal can be a useful tool in helping teachers identify both personal and organisational stressors if it is conducted in the right manner. Appraisal can provide opportunities for teachers to indicate their needs; receive constructive feedback about all aspects of their performance, being able to identify their training needs; think about evaluation procedures, having the opportunity to update their job description; being able to voice their concerns about all aspects of school life, identifying their strength and the areas which they need to work on; receiving recognition for their achievements, feeling valued. This can also help the organisation to:

- undertake an up to date skills audit, which can help current and future planning;
- identify whole school as well as individual training needs;
- help assess past and future performance.

Appraisal should be linked to inservice training provision. Teachers, especially those who feel trapped due to the reduction in promotional opportunities, need a clearly defined programme of continuing professional development.

Now try Activities Three to Eight.

ACTIVITY THREE

In groups decide on your training needs. Do not forget to cover individual, departmental and school needs. One school in the Greater Manchester area organised an inservice day at a health farm. Remember it is essential to manage all forms of stress.

ACTIVITY FOUR

What connected with the school environment causes you to feel stressed?

_____

_____

_____

_____

_____

_____

_____

_____

In small groups discuss what improvements you can make. There will be some! Even small changes can improve stress levels significantly.

ACTIVITY FIVE

Does your school offer anything extra for the health of the staff? For example, some commercial organisations offer fringe benefits to their staff often in the promotion of good health, in the form of fitness clubs, counselling, dietary advice, *Weightwatcher*-type activities, swimming, badminton facilities.

Would you like these type of activities to be organised? If so, what would you like to happen?

_____

_____

_____

_____

ACTIVITY SIX

As a whole school staff work out a stress reduction policy for the school. Remember all staff should be involved in this activity.

ACTIVITY SEVEN

Develop a school stress reduction plan. Take into account the needs of individual staff and the need for the whole school staff.

ACTIVITY EIGHT

What sort of self-help groups and networks could you establish in order to help in the reduction of stress? Examples might include: women's support groups, social groups to visit the theatre, cinema etc, cross-school discussion groups.

1. _____

2. _____

3. _____

4. _____

5. _____

4

Improving Communication
Networks in Schools

Many teachers cite poor communications in schools as a cause of stress. They also say that lack of general and specific information, lack of knowledge about what is required of them and lack of knowledge and participation in decisions are other major causes of stress. We think that it would be useful for whole school staffs or, in the case of large schools, for individual faculties to look at ways in which they communicate and we suggest **Activity One** (page 51) as a possible way of doing this.

Schools have many different methods of communicating information. These might include various types of meetings, notice boards, daily/weekly/monthly bulletins, daily staff briefings, whole school assemblies, copies of minutes which are regularly circulated etc. Many schools spend a considerable amount of time designing communication systems but seem not to spend time evaluating their effectiveness or attempting to design systems which fit better within the school organisational culture and structure. For example a 'top down' (*bureaucratic culture*) system might be appropriate for some schools and some types of information, but a team-based (*task culture*) system might be more appropriate in other cases.

Teachers need to feel that they are an important and integral part of the school teaching and learning processes. Communication is a crucial part of this. We all need to know what is expected of us, what is being planned by the management, what decisions are being made that affect our work. If we do not know these things we can feel isolated and afraid. With this fear come feelings of dissatisfaction, frustration and perhaps even alienation. In order to help teachers avoid feelings of this kind we need to develop strong patterns of effective communication within our schools. Now look at **Activity Two** (page 51).

MANAGING MEETINGS

Another cause of stress which many teachers mention is the conduct of meetings in schools. The problems seem to fall into three categories: 1. too many meetings 2. irrelevant meetings and 3. poorly organised meetings.

When asked about meetings teachers will quote the following difficulties:

- they are often boring or too long;
- there are no clear start or finish times;
- chairpersons do not stick to the agendas;
- sometimes meetings are too vague and general;
- there is no clear agenda;
- people are allowed to deviate from the agreed order of discussion;
- participants become critical;
- lack of clear objectives;
- there is no advance information so participants are badly prepared;
- lack of effective participation;
- ineffective chairing;
- people do not listen.

Now try **Activity Three** (page 53).

WHAT IS AN EFFECTIVE MEETING?

A meeting is effective if it achieves its objectives to the satisfaction of the participants in the shortest possible time (Haynes, M. 1988).

When considering the idea of effectiveness there are several questions we need to ask:

> *What is the purpose of the meeting? Information or decision making?*
> *Who needs to be there?*
> *What are the objectives of the meeting?*
> *Do we need the meeting? Is a meeting the most effective way of dealing with this particular business? We sometimes have meetings because they have been timetabled regardless of need or because we do not bother to think of an alternative way of conveying the information. Sometimes a series of telephone calls or a memo might be a better way of disseminating the information.*

Meetings, when properly organised, can bring about or facilitate positive results. These may include:

- bringing teachers together;
- generating ideas;
- energising participants;
- facilitating communication;
- airing views and preempting gossip;
- sharing resources;
- preventing individuals from feeling isolated.

Setting ground rules for meetings

Agreeing ground rules on participants' behaviour in meetings is useful. The following might be considered. It is not a conclusive list and other ideas could be added.

1. To respect everybody's contribution;
2. To listen to each other;
3. The meeting will begin and end at the agreed time;
4. Feelings and opinions will be encouraged and respected;
5. Conflict is always acceptable and often very useful;
6. Decisions will be made by the meeting by consensus;
7. Participants will help to set the agenda;
8. Decisions will be publicly available.

Encouraging participation and discussion

Many teachers find it difficult to speak out at meetings, especially if there are large numbers of other colleagues present. They can help themselves by using the visualisation techniques referred to in Chapter 10, but chairpersons of committees and meetings should also be aware of several other methods of encouraging and facilitating this process.

The quality of a discussion depends on the cooperation and the participation of the group members. The chairperson of any meeting should be particularly aware of the non-verbal signals which can indicate disagreement, boredom, frustration, wanting to speak but perhaps needing some support (see the section on Non Verbal Communication, page 48). Different types of questions can be used to generate discussion. General questions are less threatening than more direct questions and can be useful to begin discussions. More direct questions can be used later.

It should always be borne in mind that some questions may be perceived as threatening and care should be taken to use them after consideration of other non verbal signals.

Participation can be encouraged by asking individual teachers for their opinions, how they feel about an issue or by the use of open-ended questions ie ones which prompt an answer other than 'yes' or 'no'. We can ask individual teachers to summarise the discussion up to that point or the chairperson can summarise. Certain issues or points can be clarified, what has been said can be paraphrased etc. This often helps participants to clarify their own understanding, to explore ideas in greater detail and to test for consensus. The more nervous teachers can be encouraged to ask questions or offer opinions and can be given support and help to express their thoughts and feelings. The chairperson can help further by reflecting their thoughts. Sometimes it will be necessary to confront differences. This is an extremely valuable learning experience for all concerned and should not be avoided. The focus of the discussion can be shifted to the future and towards the development of action plans.

PLANNING MEETINGS

It is essential that meetings, if they are to be effective, are well planned. You might like to think about some of the following points and then try **Activity Four** followed by **Activity Five**.

Every meeting needs an objective; this is the reason for having the meeting.

Who should be invited?
Where should the meeting be held?
When should the meeting be held?
How long should the meeting last?
What aids/handouts etc are needed?
Refreshments?
Facilities for disabled people?
Preparation of an agenda
Who will chair the meeting? Who will act as secretary?
How can the meeting be evaluated?
Is there a no smoking policy?
How will the room be arranged?

Developing agendas

An agenda is a plan of the route to be taken through the meeting. It should be planned and circulated to all participants in advance, having allowed time for anybody who wishes to do so to submit an item for inclusion. The agenda should contain all the necessary information for participants to participate fully in the meeting.

The following information needs to be included:
- A title for the meeting;
- Date, time and place of the meeting;

- Details of papers etc, which are needed;
- Order in which items will be discussed;
- Time that the meeting will finish;
- Any breaks which are to be included.

It is also useful to include estimated times for each item. A specimen agenda is given below.

JOHN DALTON HIGH SCHOOL

Staff Development Committee

A meeting of the above Committee will be held on *Date* at *Time* in *Room.*

Items for inclusion on the Agenda must be handed to the Chairperson at least two days before the meeting.

Purpose of the meeting.

1.	Apologies.		C'person
2.	Minutes of the last meeting.	2 mins	C'person
3.	Matters arising.	5 mins	C'person
4.	The current financial position.	10 mins	SL
5.	Applications from staff for external courses.	10 mins	JJ
6.	Planning an in-house staff development day.	20 mins	CH

The meeting will conclude at

Now try **Activity Six**.

EVALUATING MEETINGS

It is extremely important that meetings are evaluated to ensure their effectiveness. It is by evaluation that we learn what is good about what we are doing and what can be improved. We can evaluate meetings in a variety of ways. Some ideas are given below.

1. We can stop the meeting at a certain point in the proceedings and ask for feedback.

2. We can ask participants for feedback after the meeting.

3. We can telephone a random sample of people who attended and ask for feedback.

4. The chairperson can do his/her own evaluation of the meeting.

5. We can devise a questionnaire which can be used to evaluate meetings. An example of this is given in **Activity Four**. You may need to add to or adapt this for different types of meetings.

Having worked your way through this chapter you should now be in a position to look at communication in your school more critically and to contribute more positively to meetings, both formal and informal, thus beginning to work on the reduction of stress levels frequently caused by lack of or poor communication in schools.

Now try **Activity Seven**. Attempt **Activities Eight** and **Nine**.

NON VERBAL BEHAVIOUR

If we are to behave assertively then it is essential that we have an understanding of **Non Verbal Communication** or body language. When we communicate we use two main channels; the verbal and the non verbal. By far the most important of these is the non verbal channel as we communicate more non verbally than verbally. As assertive teachers, we need to speak out firmly and clearly. This means we need to give the message we wish to convey with our whole bodies. We need to become aware of the whole message that we give. Non verbal messages can either reinforce or be incongruent with our verbal messages. We often get the words right but our body language or tone of voice can give other, stronger messages. When teachers are angry they often soften the message by smiling. When they say no to an unreasonable request they often shuffle uneasily and look away from the other person, thus indicating that they are feeling uncomfortable in the situation. If we feel assertive our whole body will convey that message as body language emerges spontaneously from how we feel. It is possible to unlearn body patterns and to modify our Non Verbal Communication. We can learn to maintain better eye contact, or to stand facing somebody without using inappropriate bodily gestures. In order to change our body language we need to first of all be aware of how we use our bodies to convey information. We often contradict our assertive responses by inappropriate non verbal behaviours. We smile when we say 'no', or when we are angry. This gives an inconsistent or mixed message. It is important that we can read and understand these signs. Some body language can indicate aggression, pointing in a threatening way, but care should be taken not to misinterpret this. We always need to be aware of what it is that we are communicating.

Cultural differences
It is extremely important that we take into account cultural differences in non verbal communication. One of the most common differences is body distance (or proximity). British people tend to stand at a comfortable distance of about 50 cms from each other, whilst Japanese people stand much closer. To British people, somebody standing too close to them can often give messages of intimacy. This may be misinterpreted by people from other cultural backgrounds. Another common problem for teachers in this area is the duration of eye contact and whether it is in fact acceptable for some cultures to have eye contact at all with groups like teachers. In some cultural groups this would be considered to be impolite. Try this out in **Activity Ten**. Remember that a comfortable distance for you might not be the same for all your colleagues or students. This might be a useful area to look at on a school-based inservice training day.

Non verbal behaviour and characteristics
These include the following:

- Facial expressions;
- Eye contact;
- Gestures;
- Body orientation;
- Body distance;
- Appearance;
- Tone, speed, pitch of voice. (These are obviously not strictly non verbal but are often included in a list of this kind.)

The mass media have helped to popularise the concept of non verbal communication. This has had both good and bad effects; good in the sense that it makes a great many people aware of some of the issues, but bad in the sense that it can trivialise them. The mass media is primarily about entertainment. When looking at and interpreting non verbal communication, it is important to remember the following points:

1. Interpret non verbal communication in terms of looking at clusters of non verbal indicators. We often hear people say 'That teacher is frowning therefore that means...' When interpreting body language, it is crucial that we look at the whole person's body, not at isolated features.

2. Always look at the *context* in which the body language is being used. A man standing with his arms tightly folded and his legs tightly crossed might mean different things in different contexts, ie standing outside in the snow as opposed to standing in a warm room full of people!

3. Always take into account body language of people from different cultures and religions. Do we always interpret this correctly or do we base everything on our own culture and experience?

4. Ensure our body language is congruent with our verbal language. We can say the same words with different accompanying non verbal signs and by doing so change the interpretation. We can say 'I'm really interested in your work' with appropriate body movements, facial expressions, tone of voice, eye contact etc, but can give quite a different message with the same words said in a bored tone while looking at our watch and glancing out of the window.

Consequently when looking at non verbal communication it is important to remember the following:

- Clusters;
- Context;
- Cultures; and
- Congruence.

Finally try **Activity Eleven**.

ACTIVITY ONE

This activity is a variation on the game of 'Chinese whispers' and is a group rather than an individual activity. The facilitator and a chosen person number one meet in a room together and the facilitator gives the person information which he or she then has to pass onto the next person and so on. After the last person has received the message the whole group can be assembled to hear the message received by the last person. This is usually nothing like the original message. Any message can be used though it should contain several facts. For example 'The head has decided to give a prize of £25 for the most original idea for a design for the front cover of the new school brochure. Entries have to be submitted by Tuesday 27 June and the decision will be announced at the school sports day in July.'

At least ten people are needed for this activity. The facilitator can then lead a discussion about what we can learn about ways of communicating in organisations.

If the group wish, this activity could be recorded on video tape for future reference. This can be very amusing but should only be done with the full permission and cooperation of everyone.

ACTIVITY TWO

What kinds of communication network exist in your school and how do they affect you? These might include some of the following:

1. in order to communicate information to the whole school;

2. in order to communicate within departments/faculties;

3. in order to communicate within subject groups;

4. in order to communicate with the pupils;

5. in order to communicate with the parents;

6. in order to communicate with the community;

7. in order to communicate with the governors.

Which of these do you think work well? Which do you think could be improved?

List the factors which encourage and enable good communication with the groups you have chosen.

1. _____
2. _____
3. _____
4. _____
5. _____
6. _____
7. _____
8. _____
9. _____
10. _____

Now list the inhibiting factors which could be improved.

1. _____
2. _____
3. _____
4. _____
5. _____
6. _____
7. _____
8. _____
9. _____
10. _____

You should now be in a position to look more critically at the whole school communication pattern and to begin to suggest ways in which it could be streamlined to make life less stressful for you while ensuring that you get to know what you need to know.

ACTIVITY THREE

Make a list of all the meetings that you regularly attend.

1._____

2._____

3._____

4._____

5._____

How often are these meetings held?

What is good about these meetings?

What could be improved about these meetings?

Having considered the above, list ways in which you think they could be improved. If you are working with a group of colleagues, compare your list with others and produce a composite one which could perhaps form the basis for a discussion, either at your next departmental meeting or whole school staff meeting.

ACTIVITY FOUR

Read the section on planning meetings. Decide on the topic of a meeting that you need to plan and write down all the things that you need to consider to enable that meeting to be effective. Refer to Activity Six which is concerned with writing agendas and use this for the activity.
  Write a checklist.

1._____	2._____
3._____	4._____
5._____	6._____
7._____	8._____
9._____	10._____

ACTIVITY FIVE

Devise a checklist for planning an information meeting; ie for informing the staff about future plans for more parental involvement in the school. The decisions have already been made.

Questions:

Who would you invite?
Who would you leave out?
How would you ensure that the people who were left out obtained the information if they needed it?
How would you arrange the room? Would this be important?
What about audio visual aids etc?

How might these arrangements (some or all of them) change if the meeting were a decision making meeting?

_____

_____

_____

_____

_____

ACTIVITY SIX

Write an agenda for a meeting to discuss the planning of the professional development programme for next summer term.

_____

_____

_____

_____

_____

_____

_____

_____

_____

Consider what other supporting documents you might need and list them in order of priority.

1._____ 2._____

3._____ 4._____

5._____ 6._____

7._____ 8._____

9._____ 10._____

ACTIVITY SEVEN

MEETING EVALUATION

Details of meeting:
Title:
Date:
Time:
Place:

Please would you complete the following evaluation sheet. The information that you give will be used to improve future meetings.

How would you rate this meeting on the following points?

```
                                    LOW                HIGH
                                    1  2  3  4  5  6  7  8  9
```

1. Did the meeting meet its
   stated objectives?

2. Did the meeting meet your
   objectives?

3. Was the agenda circulated in
   enough time?

4. Was the knowledge of the
   participants fully shared?

5. Did the participants receive
   enough advance information?

6. To what extent were participants
   encouraged to join in the discussion?

7. Were decisions made by consensus?

8. What follow-up was decided?

- -

- -

9. What was good about the meeting?

- -

- -

- -

- -

10. What could be improved about the meeting?

- -

- -

- -

11. What action will you take as a result of the meeting?

- -

- -

- -

- -

ACTIVITY EIGHT

Work out some room designs for the following types of meetings:

1. a small group of women teachers meeting as a stress management support group.
2. a full staff meeting where the head will give information about the whole school stress policy and answer questions.
3. a discussion meeting at faculty level to discuss the arrangements for examinations.

Where would you place any audio/visual aids that you might need?

Would you serve refreshments?

Any other considerations?

ACTIVITY NINE

Look at the list of meetings that you generated in Activity Three. Is it necessary for you to attend all of them? Decide on a meeting that you do not have to attend in person and work out a way of being able to obtain the information that you need without spending time being physically present at the meeting. This might include delegation, making sure that the minutes are circulated in advance of the next meeting and that you find a space to read them, making a regular spot for a report from the staff representative in your own timetabled meetings, getting the representative to write a memorandum, etc.

ACTIVITY TEN

This activity is a paired one. Stand very close to your partner. Indeed, stand nose to nose and then have a conversation about one of your hobbies or interests.

How did you feel? Did you find this easy to do?

Now repeat this activity but stand as far apart as you can, in the space that you have available and carry on with your conversation.

How did you feel? Did you find this easy to do?

Next repeat this activity standing at the most comfortable distance for you and continue your conversation.

How did you feel? Did you find this easier or more difficult than the previous activities?

People who are deaf stand a long way apart when communicating in sign language. Unlike hearing people who do not need to be able to see each other when speaking, deaf people need to be able to see the whole person when communicating.

ACTIVITY ELEVEN

Choose a member of your staff whom you think is a really effective communicator. Observe his/her body language. Does he/she always give congruent messages?

Now choose a member of your staff who you think is *not* an effective communicator. Observe his/her body language. Why do you think he/she is not effective? Make a list of inappropriate body language.

5

Managing Time

'Working smarter not harder is the real goal of effective time management.'

(McKenzie 1970; cited Richards, 1987 p73)

HOW IMPORTANT IS TIME MANAGEMENT?

Time is a valuable and unique resource which, unlike money, can't be saved for another day. Once it's gone, it's gone. Time is irreplaceable and has no substitute. You can't borrow or steal time or change it in any way; all you can do is make the optimum use of the time you have. For most teachers it seems to be the least understood and the most mismanaged resource they have. When one visits schools the most frequently heard complaint is that of lack of time. In a recent study of school management and organisation (Torrington and Weightman, 1988) the authors concluded that teachers were not managing their time as effectively as they might.

Not everyone experiences time in the same way. Sometimes time can appear to move slowly, for example when you are bored, or waiting for something to happen. It can appear to move quickly when you are fully occupied, interested in what you are doing or busy enjoying yourself. Sometimes it can appear to accelerate, for instance the second part of a holiday seems to go past more quickly than the first. This may have something to do with our sense of perspective. When one is young a year can be a very long time; at fifty the years seem to pass by more quickly. You cannot manage time; in fact, there is only one thing that you can manage and that is your own use of time. Lack of time is not the problem for most teachers; it is rather, a symptom. A symptom of objectives which are unclear, of priorities which are not properly allocated and of plans which are poorly thought through. Time management is really about self management. It is about how you do your job and how you live your life. So, how do you actually manage your time? What is it that stops you being a more effective teacher? **Activity One** will focus your attention on this aspect of your self management at work.

Below is a typical list generated by teachers and health professionals who have attended a past seminar. Though it is not complete it may well bear some resemblance to your list. Compare the two lists.

Non-urgent telephone calls;
Casual visitors (without appointments);
Ineffective meetings;
Delegation without trust;
Lack of communication;
Work overload by self/others;
Putting things off;
Interruptions;
Bureaucratic form-filling;
Unsolicited mail;
Faulty equipment (video recorders, overhead projectors);
Travel between buildings, sites, etc.

Many of these issues will be addressed in this chapter.

STEPS TO GOOD TIME MANAGEMENT

Essential steps to good time management are:

- **Wanting**: to use time more effectively;

- **Planning**: what needs to be done;

- **Organising**: what needs to be done;

- **Doing**: what needs to be done;

- **Monitoring**: what *is* being done;

- **Evaluating**: what *has* been done.

Making the decision to manage our time is similar to us deciding to lose weight or to stop smoking. It will only be effective if we really are serious and want to do it. We need to spend time planning and organising what needs to be done and how we are going to do it. We then need to follow it through with action. For our strategies to succeed we will need constantly to monitor and evaluate the process. It is wrong to think that we have to look busy all the time. It is crucial that we take time to think and to plan. The first stage is to analyse exactly how we spend our time and then to decide if we use it in the best way for us.

CIRCLES OF SATISFACTION

This presents a simple way of looking at how we spend our time. We can spend it in three main ways: **choice, maintenance**, and **sold**:

1. **Choice time**: This is how we chose to spend our time.

2. **Maintenance time**: This is the time we spend maintaining ourselves, our children, our pets, our home, sleeping, washing our hair, etc.

3. **Sold time**: This is the time that we spend earning our living, ie teaching and doing work connected with teaching, marking, attending meetings, parents evenings, etc.

NB: These are not completely separate categories. Some activities could fall in more than one circle.
     Now try **Activity Two**.

KEEPING TIME LOGS

Completing the circles of satisfaction can indicate to us in very general terms that we would like to change the way in which we spend chunks of our time. However, having made the decision to change, we need to make a detailed and accurate analysis of how we actually spend our time. For this we can use a *time log*.

It is impossible for us to remember exactly how we spent a day, a week, etc. We cannot remember accurately all our telephone calls, our answering of letters, the interruptions, the impromptu conversations that we experience without keeping an accurate log of all the activities we engage in or all the tasks we undertake. Before we can decide whether we are spending time on the right things, we need to know exactly how we are using our time. Some time-wasting activities are highly visible and can be intensely irritating. Others, often more pleasant jobs, can cost us many hours a week but would probably not appear on your list of time-wasters. The first step in improving any system is to get accurate information on current performance. Analysing the way you actually spend your time by means of a time log can often help you to identify the real problems. Draw up a sheet on which to log your use of time, such as the one given in **Activity Three**. Carry it with you throughout the day and note the start and duration of *every* activity. Make sure that you record events as they happen as memory can be unreliable. It may seem to be rather a tedious exercise and you may discover sometime during the first day that you have entirely forgotten about it. Continue; with practice it will become easier. Most teachers find that the process of recording their use of time helps them to become more efficient before they have even begun to analyse their results.

When you know what you are spending your time on, you can compare it with the way you choose to spend it in the circles of satisfaction in **Activity Two**; that is, the way you would want to be spending it. Most teachers spend their time far less effectively than they think they do, so time logs can be a salutary experience for them. Time logs can sometimes be the catalyst that can persuade a teacher to make some radical changes to his/her working practices. It might be an excellent place to start the search for greater personal and effective self management. **Activity Three** will help you to complete a time log. **Activities Four** and **Five** will help you to analyse further how you spend your time at work and to decide what changes you would like to make.

ESTABLISHING OBJECTIVES AND PRIORITIES

If we look at our official job description we will find that our jobs can be broken down into a number of key areas. These could better be expressed in terms of main aspects. In addition to analysing your time log, you need to decide on the main aspects of your job. What are you employed to do? What are the activities that make up your job? Make a list of these 'main aspects'. They should consist of no more than nine areas, two of which should be non-job related. Now try **Activity Six**.

After identifying your 'main aspects' you will need to specify your objectives for each of them. Objectives tell us, and other people, what we hope to achieve. Without clear objectives we often fail to complete the job in hand. To enable you to identify your objectives try **Activity Seven**.

After we have decided on our objectives, we need to prioritise them. Which objectives are most urgent? Where do we need to start? When establishing objective priorities we need to take account of the following:

- How urgent is it? When does it need to be completed?

- How important is it?
  – to you?
  – to the LEA?
  – to the school?

- to the governors?
- to the staff?
- to the parents and the community?
- to the pupils?
- to others?

Is it an objective which has been imposed on you, for example an instruction to complete a task by the head teacher, or is it an objective which you have chosen to do, for example to encourage greater involvement of parents in understanding the curriculum?

Look at your list of objectives and rank them according to the checklist.

Making objectives more manageable
Some jobs we keep putting off as they are too big or complicated to tackle. In order to manage these we need to break them down into small manageable parts. These we call *tasks*.

Developing tasks from objectives
Main aspect: Administration with responsibility for marketing.
Objective: To conduct an internal and external market research audit.

Objective broken down into discrete tasks
1. Conduct a survey of parental satisfaction with the school.

2. Construct a questionnaire to send to parents.

3. Make arrangements for its distribution and collection.

4. Analyse the returned questionnaires.

5. Publicise the results.

6. Arrange a meeting with parents.

and so on.

When you have listed all the tasks for each objective, check that:

1. Each is a manageable 'chunk' and can be completed fairly quickly, for example, in a meeting or in one or two non-teaching periods.

2. That you can attain your objective when all the tasks have been finished.

If you cannot achieve the above you might need to think about breaking the tasks into smaller components and perhaps adding a few extra ones.

Now try **Activity Eight**.

Other time management strategies which you might wish to consider might include all or some of the following: being able to set realistic deadlines, delegation, procrastination and the effective management of paperwork and the telephone. We will now consider some of these strategies in more detail.

Setting deadlines

Some teachers are unable to work effectively without setting deadlines for themselves. This is a very useful personal time management strategy to adopt. It is a good idea to build a 'cushion' into the deadline, ie to give yourself an extra few days to complete the task before the deadline expires. It may also be appropriate to use this strategy when delegating work to others.

Delegation

We need to ask ourselves whether we delegate as frequently as we might. What delegation means here is the giving of real responsibility to members of staff lower down the school hierarchy than ourselves, instead of just giving them jobs to do. Teachers must be trusted to make decisions about whether, what and how to do things – not just given the work of filling in lists etc. We should not be afraid to delegate work and we should not believe that we are the only people who can do the particular task. We need to think again and learn to delegate in the interests of making the best use of our time.

Dealing with paperwork

When dealing with paperwork we should, at all times, avoid chaos and clutter. For example, when we sort our post we should finish the job and not avoid certain letters because they come in brown, boring envelopes. We must start by throwing away any useless circulars or junk mail and organise a system whereby post needs to be sorted only once. The golden rule is to handle mail once only, and either discard it or write a reply immediately, if a reply is needed. Sometimes a telephone reply might be faster.

Meetings

We should look at the communication processes in our department or school. Do we really need to go to every meeting? Can we organise a system so that one member of the team will attend the meeting and will report back to the rest? Do we really need to hold all those meetings or would a memo be a more appropriate way of communicating information? For further help on the conduct of meetings and communication in schools see Chapter Four.

Telephone calls

We can't stop all telephone calls, but we can control the amount of time that we spend on them. We can be selective if we have somebody else available to answer the calls for us or if we have the use of an answering machine. It is surprising how many people do not find it necessary to speak with us when we don't take the call personally. Always keep calls short and plan what needs to be said.

Procrastination

Procrastination is known as the thief of time. Sometimes we put off doing things until they become so urgent that they really have to be done, even when there is something more important on the agenda. We make lists and always start with the things that we like to do rather than prioritise items in such a way as to make our workload more manageable. To deal with procrastination we need to set ourselves deadlines and stick to them. Promising ourselves a reward when we've finished can also be helpful. Breaking your job into small manageable tasks, as already described, can be useful and asking somebody to check that you have finished can be encouraging.

To see whether or not you are a procrastinator try **Activity Nine**.

Long-term wallcharts

These are usually associated with school-orientated activities. However, they are useful for individuals to keep as well. Deadlines can be transferred to a wallchart on a termly, monthly or yearly basis. This gives a visual display of heavy workload periods and a good overview of work which is to be completed.

Having worked your way through this chapter you should now be in a position to plan, organise and manage your time in such a way as to cause you the minimum of stress. The final activity will help you to create an action plan for better time management in the future. Now try **Activity Ten**.

Remember, if our time management is a cause of stress to us then we will only relieve this stress by thinking through what it is we need to change and then by taking action to change it. Sometimes a minor change will make a world of difference to us.

ACTIVITY ONE

Write down a list of your time wasters at work. What are the things that stop you being more effective in school? Fill in your list on the spaces provided.

1. _____
2. _____
3. _____
4. _____
5. _____
6. _____
7. _____
8 _____
9. _____
10. _____

ACTIVITY TWO

This activity can be undertaken either as an individual or in pairs.

Draw two circles. Label the first circle, 'How I actually spend my time' and label the second 'How I would choose to spend my time.' Next divide the circles into segments, each segment representing as nearly as possible your current and ideal use of choice, sold and maintenance time.

Compare the differences between the two circles. If you are doing this as a paired activity, discuss with your partner the decisions that you have both made. What does this tell you about how you would really like to spend your time?

Now think of how you can change the way in which you spend time. You need to realise that you can make choices. Through these choices you can change your use of time. As you read the chapter, different ways of doing this will present themselves to you.

An example might be the following: When I get home from work, I invariably watch the ITN News Bulletin at 5.40pm, followed by the BBC News at 6.00pm. I do not need to watch two consecutive news bulletins, so could create more time for other things during that hour. This is a very simple example of how I can change my use of time.

ACTIVITY THREE: COMPLETING A TIME LOG

Some time logs that you may have encountered previously may have fixed time slots for you to fill in, but we believe that a better way is to use the format shown below. Everything that you do is important and needs to be taken into account when completing the log.

TIME LOG

START TIME	DESCRIPTION OF ACTIVITY	LENGTH OF TIME TAKEN
8.30	Made coffee and collected post	6 mins
8.36	Answered telephone	
8.43		

After completing the time log you will now have a better idea of how you are actually spending your time, and should be in a position to use the information to manage your time in a more creative and effective way. For example, it is a good idea to do your important tasks when you are at your most productive. You need to know when your energy peaks are. Plot your energy cycle throughout the day. Do the routine and boring jobs when you are in a low energy state.

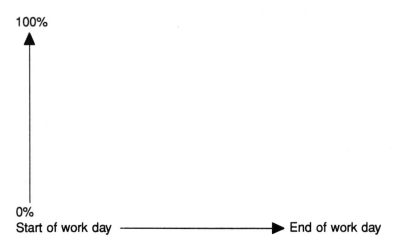

100%

0%
Start of work day ⟶ End of work day

ACTIVITY FOUR

Analysing our time gives us more control over it. We can look at the analysis under three main headings suggested by Haynes (1987):

1. Discontinue low priority tasks or activities.

2. Find someone else to do some of your work.

3. Be more efficient at what you do.

Now look at your time log and attempt to analyse it under those headings. You could start by asking yourself some questions. Some examples have been given below to get you started, but you will need to generate others for yourself as you work through the activity.

1. *What is my main problem?*

2. *On what or on whom am I spending too much time?*

3. *On what or on whom am I spending too little time?*

4. *Do I need to attend all the meetings that I currently attend?*

5. *Can I cut down on travelling time?*

6. *Could I travel to work by a different means?*

7. *Do I know which part of the day is my best time for creative thinking?*

8. *Could I delegate any of the work?*

and so on.

The activity which follows will enable you to initiate changes based on the Haynes three point categories.

ACTIVITY FIVE

Using the data gathered in the previous activity make a list of the changes you would like to make.

ACTIVITY	ACTUAL TIME SPENT	TIME I WOULD LIKE TO SPEND	HOW I PLAN TO CHANGE

ACTIVITY SIX

Work either as an individual or in pairs to establish the 'main aspects' of your job. A good way to do this is to explain, or imagine that you are explaining, in five minutes, your job to a complete stranger. This means that you will have to use very general terms and the intense focus will help you to identify your 'main aspects'.

1. _____

2 _____

3. _____

4. _____

5. _____

6. _____

7. _____

8. _____

9 _____

10. _____

Examples of 'main aspects' might be: teaching, administration, parental and community involvement, and pastoral duties.

When identifying main aspects it is important to make sure that you cover all the areas of your work, and to ensure that there is no overlap in each area.

ACTIVITY SEVEN

Again, as an individual or in pairs generate a list of objectives for each of your 'main aspects'. The following shows how this could be developed, taking as an example the objective of marketing a school.

Main aspect: Administration with responsibility for marketing a school.
Objectives: 1. To generate a school policy on marketing.
2. To conduct internal and external market research.
3. To update existing school brochures.
and so on.

ACTIVITY EIGHT

From the list of objectives that you have developed select one of them. Make a list of all the tasks which need to be completed in order to achieve the objective. Next, estimate the time that it will take you to complete each task and record your deadlines. Repeat this process for all your objectives. You are given guidance in the text of this chapter on how to develop tasks from objectives.

ACTIVITY NINE

Are you a procrastinator?
   The following activity is designed to determine whether or not you are a procrastinator. Give yourself marks as follows:
strongly agree = 4, agree = 3, disagree = 2, strongly disagree = 1.

1. If I think that the situation may be unpleasant, I think of ways of avoiding tackling people.
2. When faced with a task which I do not like, I need an urgent deadline.
3. Before I really start a major task, I feel that I need to clear up all my other tasks.
4. It is always possible for me to find a reason for not doing a demanding job.
5. I find myself too easily disrupted by day to day crises in teaching.
6. I do not always follow up action points which have been decided at a meeting.
7. I do not often use my non-contact time for preparation or marking.
8. When I encounter a part of my job which I do not like doing, I try to persuade somebody else to do it.
9. I frequently find myself under too much stress to deal with difficult tasks in school.
10. I find it difficult to make up my mind when a decision has to be made which will not be popular with other people.

Add up your total marks and score the activity as follows: *0 to 20 = You are not a procrastinator. 21 to 30 = You tend to put off tasks. This is not a major problem for you but you should pay some attention to your time management skills. 30 plus = You have major problems in procrastinating, and need to devote more time to putting this right if you are to manage your time better.*

ACTIVITY TEN

Developing action plans

If we are really serious about managing our time it is important to develop an action plan. You could use a sheet like the one following.

ACTION PLAN

	POINT/ISSUE	ACTION	WHEN?
1.			
2.			
3.			
4.			
5.			
6.			
7.			
8.			
9.			
10.			

6

Assertion

Assertion is one of the most widely used individual techniques in managing stress. It is a communication skill which can be acquired. We can gradually learn to choose how we behave in certain situations, like the times when we think 'If only I'd said... if only I'd done ...'.

Why aren't people assertive? Often teachers are afraid that it will make them appear pushy, or that other people will be upset or that acting in this way will make the situation worse. We hope that as you work through this chapter and the activities that you will realise that assertion is none of these. Instead it will help you to communicate in a more direct, open and honest way, rather than bottling up the feelings and tensions that you often experience and which can cause you stress.

People's behaviour generally falls into four categories:

1. Assertive
2. Aggressive
3. Passive
4. Manipulative

Behaving aggressively involves engaging in a 'win/lose' situation, where we intentionally set up a situation where someone has to win and the other person has to be wrong or lose. Aggressive actions are those which try to put people down or make them feel stupid. It may help you to feel powerful but generally makes others feel humiliated and hurt and in the end can lead to isolation and a desire for revenge. People who are behaving aggressively are aware of the competitive element in communication and can never afford to listen to other people's points of view as their only concern is to win at all costs. When confronted with a difficult situation they will respond with an attack.

Behaving passively involves people becoming immersed in self pity, always being apologetic and generally appearing to be lacking in self-worth. These people lack self confidence and believe that other people's needs are far more important than their own. This type of behaviour can lead to increasing anxiety. Short-term feelings of relief at having avoided conflict are fleeting. Conflict is healthy, providing we use it as a learning experience and resolve it. People who are passive refuse to accept anything good about themselves and are continually putting themselves down. They avoid making decisions for themselves and often cry when faced with any confrontation. Others frequently feel guilty because they can't help the passive individual to feel better. This sometimes turns to frustration and results in avoiding tactics.

Behaving manipulatively involves storing our aggression until later and then directing it at somebody else. It can also be used to manipulate others in order to get what we want. This behaviour might have short-term advantages but in the longer term we might find there is added stress because we did not deal with our anger at the proper time. Many people, as they get to know us, will probably spend less and less time with us. Manipulative people have a very low self-esteem and need to be in control and use guilt to manipulate people to get their own way. In this way they are able to avoid rejection.

These behaviours are stereotypes and need to be treated as such. Nobody has full control over their own behaviour. We will all recognise in ourselves elements of each of these. The important thing is to be aware of them and this may be the beginning of a desire for change.

As Dickson (1982) says:

'To recognise is not to blame. No one is at fault; each of us has simply learned to cope in the best way we could, given the circumstances at the time. Once we can let ourselves off the hook of feeling bad or guilty about our behaviour, we can begin to see choices and make changes in our lives.' (p8)

There is a difference between choosing and reacting. We react when we would like to have done something differently. We are choosing when somebody is, for example, putting us down but we choose to ignore it. We choose when we consider a situation carefully, have examined the possible outcomes of making an assertive statement, and have decided that it is or isn't worth making it.

What assertive communication is not

Being assertive is *not* about:

- being bossy;
- being aggressive;
- scoring points;
- putting people down; or

- getting what you want regardless of other people's feelings.

There are many myths associated with assertiveness training. Many people assume that only women need it. Assertive behaviour is *not* selfish behaviour. It is not about working out what you want and then going about getting it by any means. It is about balancing our own needs and wants with those of other people and deciding what is appropriate and fair on all occasions. Sometimes we have to waive our rights as our responsibilities at that moment are greater. For example when we are on holiday with young children we might wish to go off on our own to visit an exhibition but we accept that it would be inappropriate and unfair to do so.

WHAT DO WE MEAN BY ASSERTIVE BEHAVIOUR?

Learning to behave assertively involves us in:

- learning about ourselves;
- learning to respect ourselves;
- learning and recognising that we have rights which we can use and defend;
- learning to challenge incidents which exclude some people from taking a full part on an equal basis;
- learning to express and understand our feelings and recognising that our feelings are important, as well as learning skills so that we can deal with situations more effectively;
- it is about expressing who we are and taking responsibility for how we feel, how we think and how we behave.

Assertive behaviour is about communicating clearly and effectively. It is about finding out what we feel in any situation and learning how to express this appropriately, and asking for what we want while not ignoring the needs and wants of other people.

Being assertive will not on its own change the power that oppresses people in relationships and organisations such as schools but it can at least enable individuals to challenge it. Becoming more assertive can help teachers to become more confident in many situations. Being assertive isn't always easy because it demands changes in individuals' behaviour.

Assertiveness means:
1. Being able to respect ourselves, who we are and what we do.

2. Being able to respect other people and acknowledging that they also have a right to be assertive.

3. Being able to change our minds, if and when we choose to do so.

4. Being able to make clear 'I' statements about how we think and how we feel. For example, 'I think that it is a good idea to change the format of the school brochure', 'I feel very uncomfortable with the decision.'

5. Being able to set clear boundaries ourselves. For example 'I know that you would like me to come round for a meal this evening, however I want to spend this evening quietly at home. I would like to come round at another time'.

6. Being able to make mistakes. Sometimes we will make mistakes and we know that it is OK to make mistakes.

7. Being able to recognise that we have needs and to be able to see these independently of other people. There are expectations of us in all of our roles, for example wife, partner, mother, teacher, lover, daughter, neighbour etc. We need to see our needs as independent of these other roles.

8. Being able to recognise that we have a responsibility *towards* others, rather than being responsible *for* others.

9. Being able to take responsibility for ourselves for what we feel, think and do. For example 'I feel angry when you ignore me at meetings' is far more assertive than 'You make me feel angry when you ignore me at meetings'.

10. Being able to ask for 'thinking it over' time. For example when people ask us to do something and we need time to consider whether or not to do it, 'I would like to think it over and I will let you know my decision by the end of the week'.

11. Being able to ask for what we want rather than hoping that someone will notice what we want, and complaining later that we didn't get what we wanted.

Now that you are thinking more positively about yourself try **Activities One** and **Two**.

DEVELOPING SELF CONFIDENCE

Self affirmations are a good way of building self confidence. We cannot be assertive if we are lacking in self confidence. This usually goes hand in hand with having a low opinion of ourselves. In any situation what we think and feel about ourselves affects the way in which we behave in that situation. When we feel confident we will have a positive inner-self talk which will lead to feelings of comfort and relaxation and to assertive behaviour. Negative inner talk which is often 'put downs' denies our self worth and lead to feelings of discomfort, tension and consequently to non assertive behaviour. It is important that we develop positive self talk strategies. Now try **Activity Three**.

Keeping a daily record of our achievements

When thinking about becoming more assertive it might help to keep a record to show you how much progress has been made by keeping a diary of achievements. Everything, however small, should be recorded. Remember that becoming assertive does not happen overnight and that teachers cannot behave in an assertive way all the time. Later in this chapter we state that part of being assertive means allowing ourselves to make mistakes and accepting that this is all right. Listing our successes will encourage us to go on learning the necessary assertive responses in our thinking, feelings and behaviour.

Examples of things you might include are:

● saying 'no' to yet another unreasonable request;
● being firm with your children about keeping their rooms tidy;
● writing a letter to a friend;
● being patient with a colleague.

Every interaction which you manage assertively will help to build your confidence and develop your skills.

Saying 'yes' and saying 'no'

It is important to read the section on Non Verbal Communication in Chapter Four before continuing with this chapter.

If we want to say yes it is important that we actually use the word 'yes'. If, in addition, we want to add any conditions we can say so at the same time. For example, 'Yes you can borrow my book, but only for four days. I want you to return it by next Friday'.

Now try **Activity Five**.

Saying 'no'

Many teachers, especially classroom teachers, find it difficult to say no. When asked why, they give some of the following reasons:

● they are afraid of the consequences;
● they feel that it is selfish;
● they feel that a direct 'no' without an explanation will offend and hurt others.

In order to avoid a direct refusal we employ strategies like the ones listed below.

1. Giving long explanations or apologising.

2. Soften the refusal by inappropriate smiling, hoping that everybody will still like you.

3. Using incongruent body language. When we say 'no' we often say 'yes' with our bodies by:

    - smiling inappropriately;
    - adopting a patronising approach;
    - standing still and waiting for a reply when we have said no, when it would be more appropriate to walk away;
    - looking away;
    - generally looking uncomfortable.

By standing still, waiting for the next stage we offer the person making the request a second chance to persuade us to change our minds.

Guidelines for saying 'no'

1. Say the word 'no'.

2. No explanations are necessary unless you choose to give one. You must ask yourself why are you offering an explanation. Do you actually want to give one or are you feeling guilty or anxious about saying no?

3. Make sure your body language is congruent when saying no. Maintain eye contact with the other person. Think about your voice, tone, pitch, strength etc. Above all don't apologise. 'No I'm sorry but. . .'.

4. Respond to your immediate inner feeling. If that is no, then the chances are that you really want to say no. Our inner guide will advise us. If that's not a definite yes or no we can try the following:

    - *Say that you need thinking time.* Feelings are important and we need time to sort them out.

    - *Ask for more information.* If you agree to the request – how long will it take? What does it mean for you? etc. Remember, one of our assertive rights is to change our minds. If we make a 'wrong' decision we can change our minds.

    - *Own the refusal.* Change the words 'I can't' to 'I don't want to'. It is essential to remember that when we say no we are saying no to a request, not to the person. We are rejecting the request not the person. It is important for us to acknowledge our feelings. For example we could say 'I feel bad about this' or 'I feel guilty' or 'I'm finding this difficult' as this will allow us to express our feelings honestly. If you feel the other person feels rejected it is useful to discuss their feelings with them.

Making 'I' statements and use of language

It is important that we learn to use 'I' statements. This indicates that we own what we are saying and take responsibility for it. We acknowledge that what we are saying is true of our experience and that other people may have different experiences. We have a tendency to use words like 'it', 'one', 'we' or 'you' instead of 'I'. For example we need to use 'I find it difficult to go into new social situations' instead of 'One finds it difficult to go into new social groups'. Changing verbs helps to become more assertive. The words we use can indicate whether we are feeling assertive or not. We can change 'can't' to 'won't' which indicates that we have made a positive change about what we will and will not do. If we change 'need' to 'want' we can be clear about what are our needs and our wants. What is it that we want rather than need to do? We can change 'should' into 'could', again indicating that we have a choice about what we actually want to do. It is important that we distinguish between what we 'know', what we 'imagine', what we feel and what we think when we make assertive statements. We often use 'know' when we only 'imagine'.

Try **Activity Seven**.

RIGHTS AND RESPONSIBILITIES

We all have basic human rights. If we are not very confident or have often been denied our rights we may not be able to think of what they are straight away or indeed we may find it difficult to accept them. When we have doubts about the rights of assertive behaviour it is useful to remind ourselves of these rights. It is important to remember that a part of being assertive is to accept that we all have rights but that we express them in a way which does not violate the rights of other people. (People who are aggressive always violate other people's rights.) For example, the right to smoke in public may not be an assertive right as many people who do not smoke feel that this violates their right to clean air.

Assertive rights

1. *We have the right to be treated with respect.* This applies regardless of age, class, race, sexuality, disability and gender. One of our

difficulties is that we do not always treat ourselves with respect and do not therefore think of ourselves as intelligent, capable people. Women in particular often underplay their intelligence and feel intimidated by authority figures. The messages they then give out are that they are not equal and do not expect to be treated with respect. Others may be better educated than we are but on the level of being a human being that doesn't make them better or more deserving of respect.

2. *We have the right to express our feelings, opinions and values.* Many of us find it difficult to express our feelings and suppress them whenever possible. We find some feelings are more acceptable than others. It is important that we learn to recognise what we are feeling at the time. Anne Dickson points out that the right to express feelings has three aspects; identifying and recognising them, accepting rather than denying them and choosing to express them appropriately. Some feelings are easier to accept than others, for example many teachers find it difficult to accept that it is all right to express anger (when appropriate) or to feel angry. We often bottle it up inside us and allow it to fester. Hare (1990) says:

> 'I . . . accept all my feelings now – they are part of a passing parade. I feel them, and sometimes I express them to others. I no longer censor them and I believe I have the right to feel and express them.' (p84)

We have the right to our own opinions even if they are different to most other people's. It is not a matter of being right or wrong but simply a difference of perception: we have the right to be listened to and the right to disagree.

3. *We have the right to choose to* not *be assertive.* Sometimes we might decide not to be assertive and this is fine providing that it is our choice.

4. *We have the right to say that we don't understand and to ask for more information.* When we are part of a group and everyone else is sitting there listening intently and we do not understand one word, it is often very difficult for many of us to ask for more information or indeed say that we do not understand and ask for further clarification. When we do ask we will be surprised how many other people did not understand but felt too embarrassed to ask. This becomes easier with practice.

5. *We have the right to ask for what we want.* When what we want conflicts with what *others* want we will often compromise – for the sake of a peaceful life we go along with what others want. Rarely do we ask directly and tend to go round in circles hinting and hoping somebody will pick up on our wishes.

6. *We have the right to make mistakes.* We learn by our mistakes. We are all human and fallible. As adults we punish ourselves for making mistakes. Our educational system supports this idea. Consequently we are ashamed when we make mistakes; this in turn attacks our self esteem rather than acts as a learning experience for us.

7. *We have the right to fail.* For many teachers this is a difficult one. All our training is geared to helping students not to fail, it is about passing tests and examinations etc. Once we can divorce the idea of failure of a task meaning failure of the whole person, it becomes easier and we are more able to take risks. When fear of failure becomes too great because we see it as failure of the person, we will avoid situations which might make us feel this way. For example if we equate failure with taking an examination, a relationship, driving a car etc, with failure as a person, we may never take that risk again. We must all expect to fail sometimes.

8. *We have the right to succeed.* There are some fears associated with success. How will our family and friends deal with success? Will there be some jealousy? Will others find it threatening if we are seen to be successful? Will we be able to handle the extra responsibilities and will we be able to live up to other people's expectations? Yet we have the right to succeed . . . and if we believe this, we will find ways of working through and managing our fears.

9. *We have the right to change our minds.* We often make decisions that we think we 'should' make, decisions that we think are expected of us by other people. As we learn to become more assertive this will become less frequent. However, we have the right to change our minds. We can say, after giving a decision some thought, that having considered whatever it is about, we have changed our minds, we have come to a new decision. This is better than sticking to a decision that is wrong for us.

10. *We have the right not to depend on others for approval.* Many of us are too concerned with what others might think of us and therefore are afraid to express our needs, feelings, opinions, values, saying 'no' and to standing up for our rights. How often do we hear teachers say 'What will they think of me?'. We often

fail to be assertive because we are socially conditioned from an early age to seek the approval of an adult and we continue subconsciously to seek this all our lives. Again, with practice, we can learn that if we don't get somebody's approval our world does not fall apart. Often superiors will use this fear as an instrument of control.

11. *We have the right not to take responsibility for other people's problems if we choose not to.* With our rights come matching responsibilities. For example we have the right to make mistakes so we have the responsibility to be understanding of others' mistakes.

12. *We have the right to privacy.* This is often a problem for many teachers under stress. They need to be able to decide that they have a right to their own space, for example their own study, bedroom etc. if they choose.

With rights come responsibilities. For example, we have a responsibility to respect other people's opinions especially if they disagree with us. If we want people to listen to us we have a responsibility to listen to them. The right to make mistakes matches the responsibility to be tolerant when other people make mistakes. To be treated with respect also means always treating others with respect. We should go along with constructive criticism from others and accept that it is their right to engage in this.

Now try **Activities Eight** and **Nine**.

NON VERBAL ASSERTION

Before going on reread the section on Non Verbal Communication in Chapter Four.

Eye contact
If we are able to look a person directly in the eye this can greatly reinforce the message. How we look at somebody indicates how we feel about ourselves and what we are saying. For example if we look away it can often communicate embarrassment, or our eyes can convey hostility or friendliness. To look directly at somebody is very powerful and by looking away we are giving away that power. Eyes give very strong messages.

Facial expressions
For most people it is easier to smile than to show anger. As we have said elsewhere in the book, teachers under stress often smile when

they are angry. It is important to be able to recognise whether non verbal facial messages are supporting the verbal message. We also need to consider whether the tone and pitch of voice are congruent with the verbal message.

Posture
Changing our posture can change the way we feel about ourselves. It is also a clear indication to others about how we are feeling. If we walk into a room clutching a book or a folder to our chests, with our shoulders hunched up, it probably indicates that we are feeling anxious. How do we walk into a room? Some people creep in and hope that nobody notices them, whilst others march into the centre of the room. How we stand is also important. We need to be properly balanced whether we are standing or sitting. We can better do this by standing with our feet slightly apart. It is impossible to be assertive if we are not properly balanced.

Gestures
We often need to modify or keep our gestures under control. Many gestures convey anxiety and tension, for example playing with rings and other jewellery, clasping and unclasping hands, running fingers round the edges of collars, chewing fingers, playing with hair. Some gestures can indicate other feelings, for example tapping fingers or pens can suggest irritation and shuffling of feet can indicate embarrassment. If we become aware of this behaviour we can take steps to reduce it. We can relax our shoulders and make sure that they are in the down position; we can give ourselves time by breathing deeply (see also section on relaxation); being aware of our hands can help us to put them in a position where they won't give mixed messages of uncertainty. When we have got our argument sorted and we are standing or sitting in a balanced way, this can help us communicate in an assertive way. Simple modifications of gesture and stance can help us feel more confident and in turn encourage us to present ourselves in a more positive way.

Style of dress
If we wear a favourite outfit it can help boost our confidence. If we feel good we feel confident. What we wear is about how we feel and not about conforming to conventions.

Mixed messages
We give a mixed message when the verbal communication is different from the non verbal communication. We can say to a colleague that

we are really interested in his/her idea for developing a new course, but if, while we are listening, we are fidgeting with a pen and glancing at our watch, we give a non verbal message that we are not at all interested in what he/she has to say. This would be a mixed or incongruent message. (Remember, care should be taken not to judge this in isolation, as the receiver of the message could indeed be interested but not have too much time just then. Mixed messages should always be checked for clarification.)

Now try the activity on non verbal communication.

ACTIVITY ONE

Write down the heading ASSERTIVENESS MEANS.

Now make a list of what assertiveness means to you. If you are working as a pair or in small groups discuss what you have written.

ACTIVITY TWO

Why do you want to be assertive?

Make a list of situations in which you would like to be more assertive. For this activity take situations from all areas of your life. For example in shops (taking back some faulty goods); at home with your family (being able to tell them that you feel you are being used as their slave); with your neighbour (you feel that they make too much noise); at school (being put down by a superior) etc.

LIST OF SITUATIONS

1. _____
2. _____
3. _____
4. _____
5. _____
6. _____
7. _____
8. _____
9. _____
10. _____

Now go back and look at the list again. Write down for each situation how you think you behave. Choose from the following categories:

- aggressive
- passive
- manipulative
- assertive.

Example one: You have just bought a pair of very expensive shoes. You find that within three or four times of wearing them that some of the stitching is coming undone. What are your possible responses?

Example two: A teacher who is senior to you comes into the staff room and publicly tells you off for not replying to a note that he sent you last week. How could you respond?

ACTIVITY THREE

This activity is concerned with the exploration of inner resources. It will enable you to look at how positive self talk can lead to assertive behaviour and how negative inner talk can lead to other types of behaviour.

Think of an occasion when you felt very confident.

What was the situation?

What were your feelings at the time?

What was your inner self talk?

How did you behave because you were feeling confident?

Now think of a situation in which you experienced a lack of self confidence.

What was the situation?

What was your inner self talk?

What were your feelings?

How did you behave as a result of this lack of confidence?

How can you change this? Work out some positive self talk and how you could and will behave differently in that situation in the future.

If you are working in a pair discuss the changes you want to make. Your partner should be able to help you work out positive self talk, discuss how you will feel and how you will behave. Now do **Activity Four**.

Assertion

ACTIVITY FOUR
THINKING POSITIVELY ABOUT OURSELVES

Answer the following questions about yourself.

1. Make a list of the things you like about yourself. Write down at least five things.

_____

_____

_____

_____

2. Make a list of five things you are not so keen on about yourself and would like to change.

_____

_____

_____

_____

3. Look again at your second list and prioritise it in order of difficulty to change. (1) would indicate that this item would be the least difficult item to change and (5) would be the most difficult thing to change.

_____

_____

_____

_____

4. If you are working with a partner discuss the things you like about yourself and then discuss the things you would like to change and how you would start to change them. Start with the easiest thing to change. Through discussion of the positive points your partner will probably be able to suggest ways in which you can work on the things you want to change.

EXTRA POINTS TO CONSIDER

How long did it take you to answer question one?

How long did it take you to answer question two?

Was there a difference in the two?

Why do you think there was this difference?

Reread the section on thinking positively.

ACTIVITY FIVE

Think of a situation in which you want to say yes.

_____

_____

_____

_____

_____

Now think of some situations in which it is difficult to say no. Some examples might be;

1. Saying no to yet another meeting arranged at the last minute.
2. Saying no to a request from a colleague to borrow something.
3. Saying no to a persistent double glazing salesperson at your door.

Think of some situations that apply to you. Work either on your own or in pairs and work out what you would say and how you would say it.

DISCUSS THE FOLLOWING POINTS

Do you actually use the world 'no'?
Did you say 'no' firmly?
Did you make an excuse?
Did you apologise?
Did you give a long explanation?
Was your body language congruent with your verbal language?

Compare the two activities. Which one did you find the more difficult? Why do you think this is the case?

ACTIVITY SIX

It is important to practice saying 'no'. Take for example the following scene; a colleague asks you to cover for him yet again. You really have far too much work to do. Say 'no'.

If you are working in pairs ask your partner to work with you and to give you some feedback.

Work out what you will say.

Pay attention to your body language.

Think about your voice.

ACTIVITY SEVEN

Look at the following statements and change the 'shoulds' into 'coulds'.

I should be doing the ironing.

I really should be cleaning the children's rooms.

Next write down 10 statements where you would usually use the word 'should'.

1. _____
2. _____
3. _____
4. _____
5. _____
6. _____
7. _____
8. _____
9. _____
10. _____

Remember you have a choice. Look at the statements that you have written again and change the 'shoulds' to 'coulds' and add to the sentences the words 'and I chose to ....'

If you are working in pairs ask your partner to read these back to you stressing the 'coulds' and the choices you have made. Discuss this together.

ACTIVITY EIGHT

Make a list of what you feel are your assertive rights.

1. _____
2. _____
3. _____
4. _____
5. _____

Discuss with a partner if possible.

ACTIVITY NINE

Make a list of your responsibilities as an assertive teacher.

1. _____
2. _____
3. _____
4. _____
5. _____
6. _____
7. _____
8. _____
9. _____
10. _____

ACTIVITY TEN

Think about your own non verbal communication. What sort of non verbal communication do you use and how much do you use? If you are working with a partner ask him/her to give you feedback in this. Most people are surprised by the amount of non verbal communication that they use. If we are to learn to be assertive it is important that we first of all become aware of our non verbal behaviour so that we can then make any necessary modifications.

7

Managing Change

HOW THE INDIVIDUAL CAN MANAGE CHANGE

There is little doubt that change/transition causes teachers stress and that the effects of too much or too little exposure to it can be severe. Therefore the management of change is an important issue for all teachers and how change can be implemented is a crucial factor for consideration by all school managers.

The work of Holmes and Rahé (1967) which looks at life change events is well documented. They produced what is known as their *Social Readjustment Rating Scale*, which can give us an indication of how much change we have experienced in a 12-month period. Their work is based on the principle that changes cause us stress and that some types of change are more stressful than others. The scale consists of 43 life change events, all of which have been given a numerical value. Changes listed vary from the death of a partner, which is given the highest value of 100; pregnancy (a value of 40); change in home (a value of 20) to Christmas (a value of 12) and breaking the law on a very minor scale (a value of 11). Changes are cumulative during the 12-month period and by adding the scores together of all our life changes, we can see which category we fall into. There are three such categories:

1. a mild life crisis;
2. a moderate life crisis; and
3. a major life crisis.

Holmes and Rahé have suggested that 37 per cent of people in category one (mild), 51 per cent of people in category two (moderate), and 79 per cent of people in category three (major) showed, in their research, what they referred to as subsequent deterioration in health. Of course some changes, like divorce, might in the end prove beneficial and reduce stress. The inventory can be a useful guide to measuring potential stress in one's life over a period of twelve months, and if you are planning a number of changes it could be advantageous to spread them out over a longer period. For example, getting a divorce, moving house, taking on a large mortgage, having a relative to live with you etc. might not be a good time to also change your job!

During our lives we undergo many changes. Teachers, over the last ten years, have experienced numerous new initiatives, many of which they have perceived to be largely irrational and unwarranted. They have found that these, and in particular the rate at which change has been introduced, have proved to be extremely stressful for them. Some of the changes have included:

- the introduction of the National Curriculum;
- assessment and testing;
- LMS;
- greater accountability to parents and the local community;
- political interference in the teaching and learning processes;
- the demise of local democracy in education.

We should remember that:

> '...radical change in itself is a source of stress and its possible effects and consequences for schools need to be positively managed.'

> (Health and Safety Commission, 1990, p9)

The same report points out that how we view the change is crucial. Some staffs see changes in the management arrangements in schools as a great opportunity to learn and to practice new skills. Others see these changes in a more threatening and less than positive manner and feel that they are being asked to perform tasks for which they have had no training, or that their job descriptions have been substantially altered without sufficient consultation.

Barrie Hopson (1983) has done a considerable amount of research focusing on how transitions affect people. He suggests that all change or transition creates some stress, even that which society considers to be positive such as parenthood, or the winning or inheriting of large sums of money. He suggests that transitions follow a cycle of feelings and reactions that are predictable and fall into seven phases. It is important that we understand what happens to us when we experience change and looking at these phases may in fact help us to do this. If change is stressful, it will be of help to us if we can understand what is happening to us, why we behave as we do and why we feel as we do. The seven phases are as follows:

1. immobilisation;
2. minimisation;
3. depression;
4. acceptance of reality (letting go);
5. testing;
6. search for meaning;
7. internalisation.

We will now look at these phases in more detail.

1. **Immobilisation**: During this stage we experience a sense of being overwhelmed. We are unable to plan ahead, unable to think and reason clearly and appear to be 'frozen up'. The degree to which we feel this depends on the expectations we hold and how familiar the transition state is. For example if we have very positive expectations when, for example, entering into a new partnership then we experience this stage very slightly if at all. If we have negative expectations then this stage can go on for a long period of time and can be experienced very deeply. This indicates how important it is for us to be fully informed about reasons, rate of progress and rationale for any changes and indeed to be fully involved in the decision making process.

2. **Minimisation**: At this point we all attempt to minimise the change. We try to trivialise it and sometimes to deny that the change even exists. Hopson sees denial as an essential part of the reaction to crisis as it gives time and space and acts as a temporary retreat from reality, while we regain our strength to face the new situation which has often been forced upon us. Most of us could equate this with what we would consider to be a very serious transition, for example, the death of somebody close to us. However this also applies to a greater or lesser extent with all transitions. We have not been given the time in the last few years to make these changes, and many of us have not appreciated the fact or have indeed been too stressed ourselves to take the time to care about colleagues who are perhaps still at this stage when we ourselves have moved on.

3. **Depression**: Eventually the realities of the change become apparent to us and we can no longer deny them. This leads to depression which is often the result of feelings of powerlessness. We will sometimes experience very high energy levels at this time, often characterised by anger, before we slip back into periods of feelings

of hopelessness. This dip comes as people begin to realise that there has been a change and it is apparent even when the change (like getting married, forming a new partnership etc.) is brought about voluntarily by ourselves. We become frustrated as we try to manage new life requirements, new relationships and so on.

4. **Letting go**. Letting go is where we finally decide to accept the change and we start to unhook ourselves from the past. A clear letting go is necessary as this indicates that we have recognised that the change is here to stay.

5. **Testing**. During this stage we have a great deal of energy as we test out the new situation, new behaviours, new life styles and new ways of dealing with the change. As we deal with the new reality we can easily become irritable and angry. This is important to remember in schools as we reach different phases of change at different times, and this could possibly go some way towards accounting for the changes in behaviour of some teachers, as they try to manage the additional stress caused by the change and the change itself.

6. **Search for meaning**: This is a cognitive process. Here we withdraw from the activity in order to try to understand the meaning of the change. We need to understand why things are different and how they are different.

7. **Internalisation**: Here we internalise the 'meanings' and incorporate them into our behaviour, thus they become part of our experience.

Rarely do people move from phase to phase as has been described above. Each person's experience is unique and his or her progress and regression through the stages is also unique. Some people never progress beyond the minimisation stage. However it is possible to help somebody who is distressed to become aware that what they are experiencing is not uncommon, that it will pass, and that there is a great deal that they can do to determine how quickly it will pass.

'There is a potential for growth arising from any major disruption or calamity. One realises this potential and moves forward towards it when one lets go and fully accepts the situation for what it is; one dies a "little death" to become larger.'

(Hopson, B. 1983, p148)

Throughout these phases morale varies, gradually falling during two and three to a low during phase four and then gradually increasing throughout phases five, six and seven. It is important for us as teachers to understand what is happening to ourselves and our colleagues during periods of change. Perhaps it will help us to be aware of and understand the feelings and behaviour of other members of staff.

Hopson compiled the following list of the effects of transitions on people.

1. All transitions involve some stress.

2. The most stressful transitions are those which are unpredictable, those which we do not undertake on a voluntary basis, and those where both the degree and rate of change are great.

3. The amount of change experienced by an individual shows a positive correlation with the amount of illness that an individual experiences. There is a higher risk of coronary disease for individuals who experience high levels of major change.

4. Stress can be reduced if individuals receive 'interpersonal warmth and support' during stressful incidents.

5. When people do not receive feedback on their attempts to manage their stress, this can cause even more stress.

In managing change it is important that we look for the positive elements in the change. We might have lost something but what have we gained? Teachers need to be helped to understand that happens to them when changes take place, to let go of the past, set new goals and make action plans for the future and be helped to see how they and their pupils can be helped to grow.

USING FORCE FIELD ANALYSIS

Force field analysis can be a useful way of looking at any changes that you want to make. It can be used on either an individual or small group basis. It works by looking at the forces both helping and hindering the change process and thus enables you to decide on a suitable strategy for change.

Guidelines for using force field analysis

1. Decide on the change you wish to make. What is your desired goal/outcome? (Single goals are required, not multiple goals.)

2. In square one in the diagram (on p95) give a very brief sketch of the situation as it is at present.

3. In square two in the diagram give a very brief outline of the changed situation that you want to achieve.

4. Make a list of the driving or the supporting forces.

5. Make a list of the restraining or inhibiting forces. (Those forces preventing or working against the change).

6. These forces can be within ourselves, within teams we are part of, within groups we are part of, within relationships we have, or they can come from within our institutions or from within society in general. Make a list of everything that will contribute towards the change you want to make. How will these items help towards the change?

7. List all the supporting forces.

8. Now list all the forces that will resist the change you want to make.

9. Assess how strong each of these forces is. Use (-) to indicate a resisting force and (+) to indicate a supporting force.

10. To indicate the strength of these forces use up to three (-) or three (+).

11. Now decide which are your strongest (most positive) driving forces? How can you make them stronger?

12. Which are your strongest (most negative) restraining forces? How can you make them weaker?

13. You will now need to:
    – decide whether you want to go ahead with the change;
    – plan the strategy for making the change. List all the necessary steps;
    – set deadlines for each of the stages;
    – make the change.

Now try **Actitivies One, Two** and **Three**.

STABILITY ZONES

The concept of stability zones was developed by Alvin Toffler (1971) who described them as: mental retreats or anchor points. These allow us to cope with the changes and pressures which we encounter in other parts of our lives. We can manage the change in many of these stability zones if one or other remains constant.

PERSONAL CHANGE
USING FORCE FIELD ANALYSIS

Summary of goal.
What is the change I want to make?

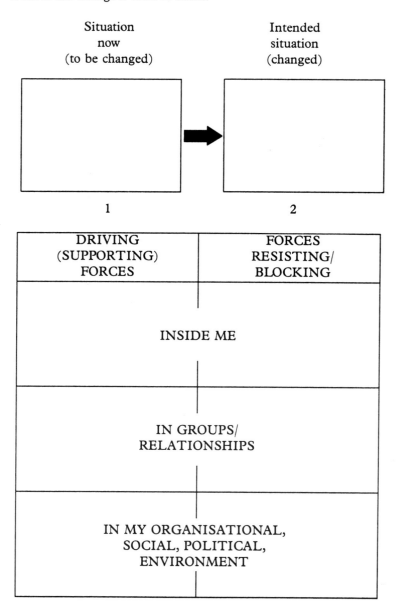

Situation now (to be changed)	Intended situation (changed)
1	2

DRIVING (SUPPORTING) FORCES	FORCES RESISTING/ BLOCKING
INSIDE ME	
IN GROUPS/ RELATIONSHIPS	
IN MY ORGANISATIONAL, SOCIAL, POLITICAL, ENVIRONMENT	

Stability zones enable us to recharge our batteries and to regain the energy necessary to make the decisions which accompany the change. They allow us to get away from the problem and to relax.

Case study
Mr B thrives on change. He has changed his job regularly over the last 15 years and is now a head teacher in a secondary school. He goes to conferences whenever possible and constantly brings back ideas which he passes on to the staff and follows up with seemingly endless energy. During the holidays he travels widely, enjoys doing new things, experiencing new sporting activities, trying out new food and drink. He is a member of many different clubs, and has a keen interest in the arts. He wears very trendy clothes and is always buying new ones. He changes his car every year.

However he is married and has been for the last 20 years to the same person. He bought a house when he was first married and still lives there. Many of his friends are the same ones he has had since he attended school and university. Although on the surface he is a man who likes change, he has very definite areas where change is rare and which provide his stability zones.

Now try **Activities Four** and **Five**.

ACTIVITY ONE

Think about the changes you have experienced in your life during the last 12 months. Make a list of them.

1. _____

2. _____

3. _____

4. _____

5. _____

6. _____

7. _____

8. _____

9. _____

10. _____

Now think about the changes that you have experienced in your school life during the last 12 months. Make a list of them.

1. _____

2. _____

3. _____

4. _____

5. _____

6. _____

7. _____

8. _____

9. _____

10. _____

Look back at your lists and classify these changes under the following headings:

- **voluntary** eg moving to a new house, forming a new relationship.
- **imposed** eg the National Curriculum, LMS.
- **welcomed** eg promotion, greater parental involvement.
- **unwelcome** eg greater administrative duties, the death of somebody close.

ACTIVITY TWO

Think of a change that you would like to make in your school or department.

What are the steps you would take in order to implement that change?

Who would you involve in the planning and at what stage?

ACTIVITY THREE

Now try using force field analysis to help you plan the identified change. Use the guidelines and the diagram given in the chapter.

ACTIVITY FOUR

When everything around us is changing we need to find some points of stability. These are often called *anchor points* and offer us mental retreats which can give us space whilst other things change. In this exercise you need to work on your own to look at your most stable areas. These can include things like:

- your home
- relationship(s)
- children
- your job
- hobby
- a favourite place
- daily routine
- others.

What are your stability zones? The categories listed below might help. You might want to use these but also to add some of your own. What you are looking for are the anchor points in your life which allow you to cope with instability, change and pressures which might arise in other parts of your life.

Ideas: How important are ideas to you? Political prisoners have been known to survive tremendous pain and deprivation because by hanging onto their ideals and values they have the necessary strength. Many teachers are committed to 'the value of education' and some have experienced great stress because they feel that education has changed so much that it now works to a different value system to the one which they hold dear.

Places: Do particular places, streets, areas of historical interest, countries, your own house provide you with your stability zone? For example, would moving house be the last straw?

Things: Are things very important to you? I worked overseas for several years. I changed jobs, left my family and friends, left my country, left my car and home but I took with me on the plane a few things that reminded me of people that I cared about and of places that I felt safe in. These were my anchor points when everything else in my life was undergoing change. (See also the case study in this chapter.)

People: Do people, friends, colleagues, family provide you with your stability zones?

Organisations: For some people the continuity of belonging to a specific organisation is the most important issue. Often teachers remain in the same school for many years as this is their main stability point when they are making other changes in their lives.

Now discuss this with a partner (if you are working with one). Where are your main stability zones?

What area would be the most difficult one for you to make changes in.

If you are to make a change in this area, how can you manage the change more effectively?

ACTIVITY FIVE

Write a set of personal guidelines for the management of the change you have decided upon in Activity Four.

HOW SCHOOLS MANAGE CHANGE

The change management model

The change management model recommends six stages as a framework for the planning of change (Kemp, 1989). These are as follows:

1. Prioritising;
2. Clarifying;
3. Creating;
4. Formulating;
5. Implementing;
6. Reviewing.

1. *Prioritising.* At any one time there are many changes taking place in departments/schools. It is important that we should not tackle too much at once so it is essential that we should decide which are the most urgent tasks and place them in order of priority. It is necessary for us to set a timescale for each of these to be completed. (Reread the relevant sections on time management in Chapter Five).

2. *Clarifying.* Having established what the change is that we wish to make we next need to clarify our objectives. We should work out who is affected by the change and who needs to be involved in its planning. We need to clarify what our outcomes are, and to be

aware that we need to set the goals.

3. *Creating*. Here we look at all the possible approaches to the task. We need to be creative and identify all the people who should be involved, the resources needed and the resources available. In addition we need to identify the driving forces and the resisting forces (see the section on force field analysis given earlier in this chapter) and see how we can change them to meet our requirements.

There are several techniques available to generate ideas. For example, brainstorming, force field analysis, discussion. Brainstorming means that a group generates a list of ideas without passing any comment. Every idea, however useless we might initially feel it is, is recorded. The aim is to generate a large number of possible ideas. Through this process an original idea might appear. When a brainstorm has been completed, the group can then place items in categories in order of importance as the members will then be in a better position to make decisions and choices. By working together group members can develop each other's ideas. Brainstorming has four main purposes:

1. *to generate a large number of ideas very quickly;*
2. *to encourage creative and lateral thinking;*
3. *to involve the whole group; and*
4. *to demonstrate that people working together can achieve more than the individual can, working alone.*

In order to generate alternative courses of action, we can make group use of force field analysis. From all the ideas generated we have the following possibilities for moving forward;

- prioritisation of ideas;
- identification of areas where there is still no agreement, discussion of selected ideas in more detail. Identification of the strong and the weak points of the topic;
- the setting out of a timetable for action;
- the development of an action plan and decisions made about its implementation in terms of who will do what, and when. One can use the same methods to identify all the available resources, people, equipment, time factors, ideas, influence, physical space, etc.

4. *Formulating*. Using the information gained in (3) above, we will now be in a position to look at the following in order to plan the change strategy:

- How will the change be resourced?
- Who will be the change agents?
- What are the costs, people, time etc?
- What hardware/software is needed?

From the force field analysis we will be able to decide which individuals will help us to implement the change and which of them will need to be persuaded.

We will now be in a better position to draw up a timescale of events. An important aspect of this is to look at the resisting forces and to see how we can overcome them/lessen them and to use the same process with the driving forces. We will need to consider how we make them stronger. We will need to take account of the extra resources that we may need. Will this involve extra financial resources? Will we need to involve people outside the school? How can we continue to motivate everyone involved? How can we keep the whole change visible to all? How do we decide on our deadlines and our timescale? It is important to remember that others have their own work and deadlines which are as important to them as your current project is to you. What part of the work can be delegated?

5. *Implementing.* This overlaps with (4) above. Here we need to consider the following:

   - How do we continue to motivate everybody? How can we ensure commitment?
   - How do we evaluate the change?
   - How do we monitor the process? Who will do the monitoring and how?
   - How can the process be coordinated and communication to all be ensured? It is essential to set up adequate communication processes to allow this to happen. Most teachers will remain motivated if they feel that they are being consulted and listened to and that their opinions are being valued.

6. *Reviewing.* Both the process of planning and implementing the change and the effects of the change need to be monitored and evaluated. It is important throughout the process to check if deadlines and tasks are being met and completed. Evaluation is crucial to see if our objectives have been achieved. We will need to decide how to do this and who will be responsible for this. It might be thought appropriate to involve an outside consultant at

this stage of the process to work alongside the staff and students.

(This has been adapted from Kemp, R. and Nathan, M. (1989) *Middle Management in Schools: a Survival Guide.*)

ACTIVITY SIX

Think about a few major changes that your department or school will need to make during the coming year.

1. _____

2. _____

3. _____

4. _____

5. _____

Encourage a group of colleagues to brainstorm these changes that the department or school needs to make.

Prioritise the changes you have identified and work through other processes of the change model.

8

Managing Conflict, Decisions and Difference

In any relationship, group or organisation there are bound to be differences. It is through difference that we grow and change. Keeping things the same can ultimately lead to stagnation. Conflict can arise when some people are not willing to listen to other's opinions, values, ideas and contributions. They can make it impossible for others to resolve differences or reach a consensus.

In organisations where there is conflict there are several ways of dealing with it:

- ignoring it;
- imposing a solution (usually from senior management);
- facilitating a process whereby all the people involved in the conflict come together to work out a solution either internally or with the help of an external facilitator.

Conflict will not disappear and merely suppressing it will usually mean that it will reappear in a different form. Not resolving issues of conflict results in stress for teachers. When a solution is externally imposed this may be done usually by people in power and is frequently done in an authoritarian or an uncaring way. In either case the solution is externally imposed and the people directly concerned in the conflict do not come up with the solution themselves. In the end it may not resolve the conflict at all.

Conflict generally occurs when people's thoughts and feelings are in conflict with those of others. Conflict resolution involves finding a new way of sorting out these differences without either being in a win/lose situation. It involves negotiation, discussion and mutual respect. This is best done by keeping the person and the issue separate. All persons concerned must be willing to listen to each other, to want to find a solution, and to be prepared to look at a range of different solutions. Now try **Activity One**.

There are a number of different ways of dealing with conflict. We offer the following guidelines which teachers may find useful.

1. Work towards a win/win situation. This means working with each other, respecting the differences between you and being committed to finding a mutually workable solution.

2. Making clear 'I' statements. This means that each person is taking responsibility for him/herself and not blaming other people.

3. Think about your non verbal communication, eye contact etc. Think about what it is you are communicating. It is important that we look at each other and listen carefully to each other.

4. What is the conflict and what do you want the outcome to be? Both people must be clear about each other's perceptions of these.

5. It is useful to choose a neutral place to sort out differences at an agreed time. It is essential that both people feel as comfortable as possible otherwise the power and dominance games come into play.

6. It is important that both people understand each other and that both ask for clarification. Brainstorming can add creativity to the solution.

7. Take one issue at a time. There is no point in confusing the situation by bringing up numerous past instances of conflict. Perceptions of this will be different.

8. Separate the whole person from the deed. This can avoid confusion and the exchange of insults.

(Adapted from Townend, A. 1985, p41)
Now try **Activity Two**.

MANAGING ANTISOCIAL BEHAVIOUR

Before reading this section it is important to reread the sections about assertive behaviour and non verbal communication. As teachers we need to be able to manage inappropriate behaviour from students, colleagues, parents etc. in an assertive rather than an aggressive manner. Examples of antisocial behaviour might include people smoking in a no smoking area; colleagues/parents being racist or sexist and making offensive remarks to you; or a member of the senior management team who behaves in a bullying or patronising manner towards you. In cases such as this it is useful to remember the following points:

- always stand your ground, do not be intimidated or threatened;
- choose the time and the place;
- give yourself time to think the issues through;
- check out the issues with your colleagues;
- maintain eye contact;
- do not make threats that you are unable to carry out;
- look at other ways of getting support, for example through the union, policy statements, from other colleagues etc.;
- do not apologise out of context or smile out of context;
- remember your breathing, always speak on an 'out' breath (see the chapter on relaxation).

GIVING AND RECEIVING FEEDBACK

In some of the exercises described in this book we have suggested that you work in pairs or in small groups. At times you will be asked to give, and in return, to receive feedback about your behaviour. We can learn more about ourselves and the effect that our behaviour has on others by receiving feedback. The following guidelines and activity are recommended. Try **Activity Three** before reading the rest of this section. See also the section on setting ground rules for meetings in Chapter Four.

Feedback is only of use if it is given in a constructive way so that individuals can learn from their experience. Feedback given in a destructive way is a waste of time as it gives the person receiving it nothing that he or she can use for learning. It can leave people feeling very negative. 'Negative feedback' can be extremely useful but it should be given skilfully and within the rest of the guidelines.

1. Start in a positive manner. We are more likely to listen to things that might be altered if we first of all hear what is good about our behaviour. Many teachers report that their colleagues are more likely to point out their weaknesses than their strengths. Criticism is usually taken to be something negative rather than something which we can learn from. It is essential that feedback be given in a genuine way. Teachers can easily pick up the appropriate management training on a short course but in practice may not be able to carry it through.

2. When giving feedback we need to avoid making general comments such as 'that was really good' or 'that was awful'. It is important

that we learn from the experience so we need to be specific. Point out what was good or not so good. For example,

> 'I liked the way in which you spoke to Carol. You obviously realised that at that point she needed some support.'

or

> 'The way you were standing when you spoke to the manager of the shop about the faulty shoes and your refund was really assertive.'

In this way we can learn from the situation as we know exactly what is good. This is equally important when giving 'negative feedback' or referring to things which might be changed. For example, refer to something which you thought was well handled first of all, before making your suggestion for change.

> 'The way you were standing when you spoke to the manager of the shop about the faulty shoes and your refund was really assertive, however it would have been further improved ... if you had maintained eye contact with him for longer' (or something else specific).

Here you refer to something which can be changed if the person wants to, thus turning the 'negative' into a suggestion which is positive.

3. It is important that we *own* the feedback. Often we hear others saying, 'You are...'. Here we are offering our opinions so we need to take responsibility for them. (In the jargon this means owning). Feedback statements would then start with words like 'I...' or 'In my opinion...'.

   The receivers of the feedback should feel that they have choices and that change has not been demanded. Feedback gives information about ourselves but should leave us with the choice of whether we change or not, and with an understanding of what those choices actually mean. It can help us to examine whether or not we want to change. When we receive feedback there are some guidelines that we can usefully follow. For example, we sometimes do not like the feedback that we get and there is a tendency to reject this immediately or to start to present an argument to counteract it. First of all it is important that we listen properly. Make sure that you understand the feedback. Check it out. Remember the feedback is one person's opinion and that you can check with others about their perceptions of you. We can ask for feedback about different aspects of our behaviour and we can decide what decisions to make on the basis of any feedback that we might get. Giving and receiving feedback is an important means of learning and self development.

Another potential conflict situation which may arise in school life is around the whole area of decision making. Many teachers feel stressed by the fact that they feel powerless within the organisational structure of their schools. A common complaint is that many classroom teachers do not feel involved in making decisions which directly affect their work. It is important that everybody in the school knows who is responsible for taking particular decisions. Here we are concerned with making decisions (choosing between two or more possible alternatives) and problem solving (which includes developing and creating alternative solutions and going through many stages in order to arrive at a satisfactory decision) (Brilhart, J. K. 1986).

Group decisions take a long time (and are therefore costly in terms of resources) and some consideration therefore needs to be given to whether it is appropriate for a group or an individual to make the decision. You may need to consider whether it might be more appropriate for somebody else with more relevant experience and skills than you to take the decision instead. However a group decision might be the best way forward in deciding certain issues which affect all staff. Group decisions have some advantages; each member brings to the discussion a body of knowledge and skills which can be shared; being present in a discussion often triggers off thoughts in people which would not happen if they were working alone; mistakes and flaws in arguments can be more easily detected; and often people are more creative in groups.

Try **Activity Four** here.

THE DECISION MAKING PROCESS

There are six main parts in the decision making process.

1. First of all we need to define the problem very clearly. As we collect more information we add to the definition and that can lead to a somewhat muddled process. It is also important to clarify who has to be involved in the decision making process and how they are to be involved. It is useful here to decide what information is needed and to set clear timescales for these parts of the process.

2. Collecting the necessary information. Here it is important to ask who will be affected by the decision and who should be consulted

about it. It is crucial that we hear everyone's views on the problem. At this stage we need to be aware of and to consider every aspect of the problem. It is very important that we clarify the definitions and the information and check to see that everyone involved understands them.

3. This stage is concerned with generating solutions. We need to generate as many as possible. This can be done in many different ways, for example in discussion with individual teachers, by brainstorming in small groups, by asking for consideration to be given to the issue in other meetings etc. A record should be kept of all possible solutions. Nothing should be rejected however inappropriate it appears at the time.

4. The possible solutions to the problem now need to be evaluated. We have to decide a set of criteria by which we can decide on the best possible way of making the decision. Some criteria may already be laid down for us by context and circumstances. Other criteria might include such things as consideration of costs and fitting in with existing school policy and philosophy.

5. We now need to take the decision. In order to do this we need to reach a consensus. It is important that the decision is recorded accurately once it is agreed.

6. The final stage is to make sure that once a decision has been reached it is carried out. Clarification about who will do this and in what timescale is essential. The people involved need to be informed and once implemented, the decision needs to be monitored and evaluated to see if it is a good decision or whether further issues emerge through discussion. Now try **Activity Five**.

Achieving a consensus

Is voting a good way of reaching a decision? It has many advantages, it is fast, discussions have a definite end point and everyone present has the right to a vote. The disadvantages include the following: it assumes that differences of opinion are inevitable and that it is the views of the majority which should count. Some people may not be committed to the decision and it can prevent or stifle creative thought. Consensus, on the other hand,

'stresses the co-operative development of a decision with group members working together rather than competing against each other. The goal of consensus is a decision consented to by all group members.'

(OU, 1990, p72)

This does not mean that everybody is in full agreement with every decision but there is enough agreement so that everyone will support the decision reached. This usually leads to greater commitment to the decision and to greater participation in the decision making process and to more creative solutions. Consensus requires teachers to be cooperative, well motivated and sympathetic to the culture and ethos of the school.

Now try **Activity Six**.

ACTIVITY ONE

This exercise needs to be completed in groups of three. Two people should carry out the role play while the third one should act as the observer and give feedback. Each participant should have the opportunity of practising each role.

Choose one of the scenarios listed below and then add one of your own.

1. A colleague insists on smoking in a very small staff room. The school has a no smoking policy.
2. A colleague makes offensive sexist or racist remarks.

In each case discuss how you would deal with this problem. What would you say? Pay particular attention to your non verbal communication.

ACTIVITY TWO

This is a paired activity. Choose a person that you would like to work with. Discuss with him or her a situation in which you experienced conflict at work. Talk about what was said to you in that situation. Remember that you want to respond in an assertive way and work towards a win/win situation rather than the win/lose situation that is so often the case.

Work out with your partner how you could achieve this and what you would say in the situation you are working on.

Refer to the guidelines for dealing with conflict.

ACTIVITY THREE

Think of a time when you were given destructive feedback by a colleague about an aspect of your work. Write down details of the incident and remember how you felt at the time. If you are working as a pair share this with your partner. Discuss with them if you think that this helps you. Could the feedback have been given in a better way?

Now think of a time when you received some constructive feedback about an aspect of your work from a colleague. What happened and how did you feel?

Was there any difference in your feelings in the two instances?

Why do you think this is?

Discuss with your partner some guidelines for giving feedback.

ACTIVITY FOUR

Think about the decisions that are made in your school.

Who makes these decisions?

How are they made? For example, by one person, by a team of people or by a committee?

ACTIVITY FIVE

Work with a partner or if possible in small groups, to look at an area of difficulty where a problem needs to be solved.

1. Define the problem.
2. Work out what information you would need to reach a decision.
3. Brainstorm ideas.
4. Make a list of criteria you would use to decide how you make the decision.
5. How would you reach a consensus? What would be a suitable method of doing this?
6. How would you evaluate the eventual decision reached?

ACTIVITY SIX

Make a list of the reasons why consensual decision making would/ would not work in your department/school. What could you do to improve the process?

Discuss this with a partner.

9

Inner Self Talk and Rational Beliefs

The principles of *Rational Emotive Therapy* can be used to manage our feelings and to help us get them under firmer control. Rational Emotive Therapy is what we say to ourselves about what is happening (that is, our inner self talk) which causes us to feel angry, happy, anxious, sad, depressed etc. rather than what actually happens to us. It could be summed up by saying that thinking precedes feeling. What we think determines what we feel. It therefore follows that if we change how we think, we can then change how we feel. A frequently used therapeutic method involves retraining people to talk internally to themselves and helps them to devise a framework to enable them to look at their irrational belief systems.

Our feelings are divided into three parts:

1. The stimulus which activates the event.
2. The thoughts or beliefs and inner self talk about the event.
3. The emotions, feelings and behaviours that result from the activating event.

Most teachers are unaware of the second of these points. Rational Emotive Therapy is concerned with moderating those of our feelings which make it difficult for us to do things effectively. It is about managing our feelings, not repressing them. In order to become aware of the second of the above points we need to listen to our inner self talk and to challenge the irrational thinking/belief.

We all have our own inner rules. Many teachers have internalised sets of rules decided for them by others. Many of these are unrealistic and generate negative feelings. To help you decide how far you have internalised unrealistic beliefs about your willingness to take responsibility for other people's behaviour you should attempt Activity One which is entitled 'Are you a rescuer?'

Now try **Activity One**.

Having worked through Activity One, you should now know

whether or not you have a tendency to jump in and rescue people. If you do and you have answered yes to a lot of the questions then you could have unrealistic beliefs about yourself and hence your work as a teacher. The main unrealistic belief we have about ourselves as teachers is probably the one that suggests that we can take on board and solve everybody's problems. We can't do this. Part of our job in teaching is to encourage and enable our students to take responsibility for themselves and their learning. Many people from the helping professions have strong 'rescuer' patterns of behaviour. There is absolutely nothing wrong with caring about our pupils but we have to make sure that we do not confuse their needs with our need for others to depend on us. This can only stifle their growth and prevent their moving towards self actualization. Underpinning the rescuer role is a strong belief that we are better, brighter and more intelligent than our students. We believe that we are indispensable and force students to become dependent on us. When this fails we become resentful or angry, feel incompetent and this leads to an increased amount of stress. Thinking about this should lead you into **Activity Two**. You will now be more aware of the nature and extent of your own irrational beliefs. You need next to consider how to deal with them.

The following are examples of irrational beliefs. They are often characterised by the word 'must' and this is often referred to as 'musturbatory thinking'. They are as follows:

- A belief that I *must* be loved and liked by everybody who is significant in my life. If I do not receive approval for everything that I do, then I am a bad person.
- A belief that I *must* always get what I want and that other people must always treat me in the way that I want them to.
- A belief that everything I do *must* be perfect. That I *must* always be competent, otherwise I am a worthless person.
- A belief that if there are problems there *must* be a quick and easy solution.
- A belief that if something is dangerous I *must* keep dwelling on it and always be anxious about it.
- A belief that I am a victim and that outside forces and other people's actions *must* be responsible for my pain and misery.
- A belief that it is easier to avoid rather than face difficult situations.
- A belief that the things I did in the past *must* determine how I feel and act today, a belief that people do not change.

We need to challenge these beliefs. Why do we need to have everyone's approval? Do I like and love everyone? So why do I need this approval? In the case of my job I try to do it well but a small error does not mean that I am a useless person. Becoming upset about someone else's problem does not help him/her and does not mean that I'm not a caring person. I can still empathise and support and help them work through their difficulties by not becoming upset. We are all human and fallible, have our own needs and sometimes don't find the 'perfect' solution. It is not our 'fault' if we make mistakes. If our plans do work that is wonderful but if they don't, it isn't the end of the world.

Some points you could look for when identifying unrealistic beliefs include:

1. 'MUSTurbatory' language, ie when our thinking is ruled by 'musts', 'shoulds' and 'oughts'.
2. Behaviour and negative emotions which are inappropriate. We cause ourselves difficulties by 'demanding', that is turning wants into demands. For example, Fred *ought* to be different, Susan *must* do this my way, Angela *should* cook eggs in butter. There are rarely rules for all occasions. It is irrational to stick rigidly to a belief without being flexible. It is impossible to insist on perfection. The world would be a very boring place if everyone were perfect.
3. Damning the whole person for a piece of behaviour. The behaviour might be bad but that doesn't mean that the whole person is bad.
4. Catastrophising. Here we use words like awful, horrible, terrible, dreadful and think that if we are not exactly as we or others think we should be, the situation will be absolutely awful, dreadful etc.

USING INNER SELF TALK IN A POSITIVE WAY

We can use this inner self talk to help to reduce our levels of anxiety. One of the characteristics of an unrealistic inner rule is to catastrophise. For example, many teachers find it difficult to give presentations to parents, a now essential part of many teachers' jobs. They get into a state of great anxiety imagining all the things that could possibly go wrong. Their inner self talk goes something like this;

'What if I completely forget what I'm saying?'

'What will I do if my voice begins to shake?'

'*What if I trip over my feet whilst walking up onto the stage?*'

'*What if...*'

Here we need to listen to what our inner voice is telling us but also to challenge those thoughts, and endeavour to change the negative talk into positive talk (see also the section on visualisation, page 00). For example we might say in answer to the first sentence 'How often do I forget what I'm saying?' If I do then I could make it into a joke. Nobody's perfect and I will always have my notes handy. Would it be the end of the world if I *did* forget what I was saying? Of course it wouldn't.

Activity Four will help you to work through a similar situation.

ACTIVITY ONE

Are you a rescuer?
Look at the following list of questions. Without thinking about them answer yes or no. It is your *initial* reaction which is important and a yes or no is required. There is no room in this exercise for uncertainty.

1. Do you feel that your pupils aren't appreciative enough of your help?
2. Do you pay more attention to your pupil's needs than to your own needs?
3. Do you feel best when you are helping other people?
4. Do you feel responsible for other people's happiness?
5. Do you have difficulty letting other people come to their own decisions or voice opinions that do not agree with your own beliefs?
6. Do you have difficulty allowing other people to take risks or try new behaviours?
7. Do you always feel obligated to respond to anyone who seems to need help?
8. Does a large portion of your job satisfaction and personal wellbeing depend on your pupils' improvement?
9. Are there personal needs of yours that are being met through your job that should be met outside of work?

Explanation of scoring
Each question that you have answered 'yes' to suggests rescuer belief or behaviour.

Source: Adapted from Smythe, EEM: *Surviving Nursing*, Addison-Wesley, 1987, pp141-142.

ACTIVITY TWO

If you are a rescuer this activity is designed to help you formulate guidelines for yourself so that you can avoid playing this particular role.

Work in pairs, if possible, to develop guidelines for each other based on the beliefs that you have identified and which need to be changed.

Try using some of the words/phrases given below.

conscientious	calm and confident	consultative
cooperative	encouraging of others	resentful
self-reliant	reluctant to delegate	resistant to change
loyal	powerful	helpless
responsible	dependent	professionally dedicated
anxious	reliable	risktaker
fearful of conflict	frightened of failure	oversensitive
frustrated	unadventurous	creative
efficient	innovative	diplomatic
practical	well organised	observant
obliging	right	wrong

ACTIVITY THREE

Study the examples of irrational beliefs given below. Think about your own irrational beliefs, then try to work out why they are irrational and how you could deal with them. Discuss with your partner if you are working with one.

Analyse any situation in which you think it would be better for you to be feeling and behaving in a more positive way.

Example
Christine is a 27 year old teacher in a secondary school.

Activating event: She has great difficulty in completing a particular task on time.

Beliefs and thoughts: I must be on top of things all the time. I must be competent all the time.

Behaviour: Feelings of anger and frustration, depression, sometimes severe panic, and an inability to concentrate so that the problem becomes worse as the stress increases.

ACTIVITY FOUR

Look at the list of irrational beliefs given in the text.

Which of them apply to you?

How can you change these?

Discuss this with a partner.

It is important to remember that this could be a very threatening exercise. Many of these thoughts and feelings will be very deep rooted and may need to be worked on over a considerable period of time.

ACTIVITY FIVE

Think of something that you have to do which causes you to feel extremely anxious. For example, giving a report at a large meeting. Record your inner self talk. Now challenge this inner self talk and rewrite it in a more positive way. If you are working with a partner discuss your answers with them. They will probably be able to help you write the answers and talk you through the situations. You may be surprised at how much you have in common.

Make a list of other occasions when you feel very anxious and repeat the exercise above. It is useful to identify the situations which cause you problems in advance, so that you can plan your management strategies well ahead.

Dealing with an excessive emotion
The more strongly we hold a belief, the more difficult it is to change it. In this case we often need to repeat Ellis's three part method (referred to earlier in the text) several times in order to get a manageable emotion. For example;

- Activating event
- Inner self talk
- Excessive emotion
- Challenge
- Manageable emotion
- Replay activating event

and repeat until the emotion is under control sufficiently for you to make an assertive reply rather than an aggressive one (adapted from Hare, p98).

Think about a time when you felt an excessive emotion.

- What was the occasion?
- What was your inner self talk?
- What was the emotion you experienced?
- How could you now improve the situation?

ACTIVITY SIX

Think of a social situation connected with your work which causes you great anxiety. Many teachers find it very difficult to take part in one of the now obligatory social events of the school, which often necessitates the teacher engaging in a variety of activities and social talk with parents, governors, representatives of local industry and other visitors. Many excellent teachers are extremely shy when not in the classroom and find this situation very stressful. The sort of inner self talk might follow these lines. *'I know I will feel anxious when I have to walk into the room to meet all these people. Everybody will look at me and will think that I'm boring and dull. As I walk into the room I know that my anxiety level will rise yet again and I will feel like running away. What will I talk about? What will I do if nobody wants to speak to me?*

Work with a partner to sort out your new inner self talk.
What other strategies could you use?
For example, arrive early so that there are fewer people that you have to face initially; decide to arrive at the same time as a colleague; use the visualisation techniques described in Chapter 10.

10

Relaxation and other Stress Reducing Techniques

In previous chapters we have looked at a number of ways in which individuals or groups can manage and reduce stress levels. Among those techniques frequently quoted in the literature of stress management are those of mental and physical relaxation. It is appropriate to look at some of these in this chapter, as teachers are now required to acquire and develop skills often more allied to business practices. One such demand, for example, is that of being required to make presentations of one kind or another, to colleagues, to parents, or to governors. This can often be a cause of stress.

RESTING

We all need to rest. How much rest we each need varies from person to person. When we become very stressed we often find it difficult to sleep. It is important that causes for this are identified but it is useful to remember that sleep is not the only form of rest. We can rest by engaging in various forms of relaxation.

> 'Rest is really "taking a break" (from our cycle of stress) and stopping activity. The body will respond by lowering the blood pressure, breathing may become slower, muscles relax and the mind empties.'

(Pearson, V. 1991 p71)

Relaxation of various parts of the body

If we can become more aware of our bodies we will be more able to judge when we are becoming tense and thus able to take control. For example when we become tense our breathing becomes shallower, faster and generally tight. Recognising this means that we are able to take control and readjust our breathing patterns. Increasing our general body awareness helps us to be more relaxed and thus more comfortable and confident in our dealings and interactions with other teachers. Becoming aware of a tightening of our muscles enables us to develop ways of relaxing them. Now look at **Activity One**. A useful way of recording periods of relaxation and evaluating their success is to keep a relaxation diary (see **Activity Eight**).

Relaxation using breathing
Becoming aware of our breathing is an important part of stress reduction. By simply concentrating on and listening to our breathing we can start to rest. This can be further developed by adopting a regular and controlled pattern of breathing by counting to the same number whilst both inhaling and exhaling, or by establishing a breathing pattern to the rhythm of a piece of suitable music. Visualisation can also be added to this.
   Now try **Activities Two** and **Three**.

Visualisation
Visualisation exercises can be used to encourage teachers to visualise themselves in situations to reflect on and learn from their experiences. They can then go on to visualise themselves in the future in a more positive way. An example that would be applied here can be found later in this chapter in the section 'Reducing anxiety in giving presentations'. Now try the visualisation ideas which are given in **Activity Four**.

Other forms of relaxation
Many other types of relaxation techniques can be explored. These include:

- aromatherapy
- deepheat treatment
- spinal therapy
- massage
- yoga
- reflexology
- meditation
- use of music, on its own or with all the above.

GIVING PRESENTATIONS

One of the most stressful situations which teachers are likely to encounter in schools is that of being required to give a presentation, whether to colleagues, governors, parents or other members of the local community. We now include some guidelines which will help you to relax and perform to the best of your ability when called upon to speak in public.

Guidelines for reducing stress when giving presentations

1. *Always plan well.* You could start this by asking yourself the following questions:
   - Where will the presentation take place?
   - How will the room need to be arranged?
   - What audio/visual aids do I need?
   - Am I using too much jargon?
   - What are my aims and objectives?
   - Who is my audience?
   - In what form do I want to have my notes?
   - Do I need any handouts?
   - How can I involve the audience? etc.

   It is essential to be well organised. This gives us the confidence to perform well.

2. *Visualise the presentation.* It is important that we learn to visualise ourselves dong the thing which causes us to be anxious (in this case a presentation) well. This means that we need to gather as much information as possible before the presentation. Find out as much as you can about the environment, visit the room if possible, obtain as much information about the audience as you are able. Visualisation helps us to bring a positive approach to the situation.

3. *Practice making your presentations.* For this you can use a mirror, a video camera or a friend to give you feedback. Reread the section on non verbal communication in Chapter Four at this point. Practice everything: how you stand, how you can best arrange your notes, when to involve the audience etc.

4. *Try to relax before you start.* Think about your breathing. Many teachers, including those who have a great deal of experience, go through a ritual before giving a lesson or making a presentation. What is important is that everyone develops ways of reducing his or her stress to levels which allow him or her to perform at his or her optimum level.

5. *Work out ways of reducing the tension in your body,* especially if you have to wait before making your presentation. Even sitting in front of an audience for some time before your contribution can help you to develop methods of relaxation, such as breathing deeply and evenly, stretching and relaxing muscles. Many

teachers have been known to suffer from extreme cramp when they stand up to give their presentations because they have been so tense during the waiting period.

During your presentation it is important to relax your body and to move around rather than stand rooted to the spot.

6. *Make eye contact with your audience.* This will give you feedback as to how the presentation is being received and to indicate to you if you need to make any adjustments such as changing pace, allowing time for questions, checking understanding and summarising.

Now try **Activities Five, Six** and **Seven.**

ACTIVITY ONE

This exercise should take about 20 minutes. It can be worked through with a trainer, a friend or friends, or on your own. You should find a suitable area, then take off your shoes and wear comfortable loose clothing before starting the exercise.

1. Find a space where you can sit or lie comfortably.

2. Now close your eyes and be aware of your breathing. Breathe in through your nose and out through your mouth.

3. Starting with your feet and working through your whole body, tighten your muscles on an 'in breath' and relax them on an 'out breath'.

4. Starting with your right foot, stretch your toes, foot and your entire leg out for as long as you can and then let it drop on the out breath. Repeat this two or three times.

5. Repeat the exercise with the toe and foot of your left leg, stretching as you breathe in and relaxing as you breathe out. Repeat this two or three times and then allow both of your legs to relax.

6. Now on to the pelvis. Lift the whole of your pelvis off the floor and at the same time tighten your pelvic muscles. Hold this for a moment or two and then let yourself sink to the floor. Repeat this a number of times, tightening your stomach muscles as you breathe in and letting them go as you breathe out.

7. As you breathe in and out be aware of taking air into your lungs and of your chest rising and falling. Hold your breath and then let it go. Repeat this once or twice.

8. Next work on your right hand and arm and your left hand and arm

in turn. As you breathe in stretch your fingers and arm off the floor, as you breathe out relax them and drop them to the floor. Repeat this exercise a few times.

9. On to the shoulders. As you breathe in lift them off the floor and hold them, let them drop as you breathe out. This is a particularly useful exercise if you suffer from tension in your shoulders.

10. Your neck, face and head are the next parts of the body on which to focus. Support your head on the floor. Tighten your facial muscles up as you breathe in and let them relax as you breathe out. Continue to do this until you feel your face becoming more relaxed.

If you have worked through this exercise properly, all parts of your body should now feel more relaxed. Check this out for yourself. If there is any part that you would like to relax more, go back and repeat the exercise for that part, tightening it as you breathe in and relaxing it as you breathe out.
(adapted from Townend, A. (1985) *Assertion Training* p32).

ACTIVITY TWO

Being aware of our breathing when using assertiveness and in giving presentations is essential. When we are feeling stressed we often attempt to speak on an 'in breath' instead of on an 'out breath' which causes us to sound as though we are not fully in control. If we learn to speak on the 'out breath' our voice sounds more controlled and it does in fact lead to us feeling calmer. Practice this and listen carefully to how you sound. If possible work with a partner to get their feedback. Reread the section on assertiveness.

This activity is best carried out with the help of a partner. On an 'in breath' try saying '*aah*'. Now repeat on an 'out breath'. Listen to and feel the difference. Discuss this with your partner.

ACTIVITY THREE

Find a piece of quiet music with an 'easy, gentle beat'. Try to regulate your breathing to this rhythm. Remember to inhale and exhale for the same length of time. Concentrate on listening to and feeling your breathing. How does this make you feel?

ACTIVITY FOUR

Visualisation one
For this exercise you should wear comfortable loose clothing and take off any footwear.

1. Find a space where you can sit or lie comfortably.
2. Close your eyes and think of a place where you have been before and where you feel happy, relaxed and safe. People often choose places like the seashore, a hillside, a park, their garden etc. If you cannot think of a place that you have been to, create one in your mind.
3. Now imagine that you are actually in this place. What can you see? What can you hear? What can you smell? Who is with you? What are you/they saying? How do you feel? Feel the peacefulness of this experience and the calmness. Let this fill your body and mind so that you feel refreshed. After about ten minutes open your eyes, stretch and enjoy the feeling of relaxation.

Visualisation two
This is a paired exercise.
Repeat the above exercise but in addition select some change that you would like to make and visualise yourself doing this. When you are ready, share this change and any experiences of the visualisation with your partner.

ACTIVITY FIVE

Think about a time when you have to make a presentation which causes you to feel anxious.
Make a list of everything that you could plan in advance.

1. _____
2. _____
3. _____
4. _____
5. _____
6. _____
7. _____
8. _____
9. _____
10. _____

If you are working with a partner discuss this list with them. Can you now add to it?

ACTIVITY SIX

Work out a relaxation procedure to last about three minutes that you can carry out whilst sitting in front of an audience.

ACTIVITY SEVEN

If you have access to a small group, prepare a short presentation of about five minutes. Ask the group to give you feedback.

ACTIVITY EIGHT

Keep a relaxation practice diary. Whenever you do some relaxation practice keep a diary of how you get on and how you feel. Use the 'before' and 'after' columns to record the amount of tension you feel. Nought represents zero tension and '10' represents very high levels of tension. Making notes on how you feel allows you to evaluate the success of the activity.

Before   After   Notes   Date   Time

_____

_____

_____

_____

_____

_____

_____

_____

_____

Bibliography

AMMA *A Review of the Research into Primary Causes of Stress among Teachers*, London, 1986.

AMMA *Stress in Teaching*, AMMA Education Conference Report, 10 October 1987.

AMMA *Teacher Stress: Where Do We Go From Here?*, London, 1987.

AMMA *Managing Stress. Guidelines for Teachers*, London, 1990.

Argyle, M. and Trower, P. *Person to Person: Ways of Communicating*, Harper and Row, London, 1979.

Bailey, D. and Sprotson, C. *Understanding Stress*, Part Three, HMSO, London, 1987.

Brilhart, J. K. *Effective Group Discussion*, Wm. C. Brown, Iowa, 1986.

Brown, M. and Ralph, S. 'From Aromatherapy to Time Management: Unorthodox and More Traditional Ways of Managing Stress', *Managing Schools Today*, 1992.

Brown, M. and Ralph, S. 'Tense, nervous headache? Combating teacher stress', *Managing Schools Today*, Vol. 1, Issue 5, Jan/Feb 1992, pp 33-36.

Cole, M. and Walker, S. *Teaching and Stress*, OU, Milton Keynes, 1989.

Cooper, C., Cooper, R. and Eaker, L. *Living with Stress*, Penguin, Harmondsworth, 1988.

Cook, R. *The Prevention and Management of Stress*, Longman, Harlow, 1992.

Cox, T. 'Editorial', *Work and Stress*, Vol. 1, No. 1, p1, 1987.

Cox, T. et al. *Teachers and Schools: A Study of Organisational Health and Stress*, NUT, London, 1989.

Dickson, A. *A Woman in Your Own Right: Assertiveness and You*, Quartet Books, London, 1982.

Dunham, J. *Stress in Teaching*, Routledge, London, 1992.

Education Service Advisory Committee *Managing Occupational Stress: a guide for managers and teachers in the schools sector*, HMSO, London, 1990.

Ellison, L. *Education Management for the 1990s*, Longman, Harlow, 1990.

Friedman, M. and Rosenman, R. *Type A Behaviour and Your Heart*, Fawcett, Greenwich Publications, Conn., 1974.

Handy, C. *Understanding Organisations*, Penguin, Harmondsworth, 1985.

Hare, B. *Be Assertive*, Macdonald and Co., London, 1988.

Haynes, M. *Effective Meeting Skills*, Kogan Page, London, 1988.

Holmes, T. H. and Rahé, R. H. 'The Social Readjustment Rating Scale', *Journal of Psychosomatic Research*, 11, pp 213-218, 1967.

Hopson, B. in Herbert, M. *Psychology for Social Workers*, Macmillan, Chapter 11, 1983.

Hoy, K. W., Tarter, C. S. and Kottkamp, R. P. *Open Schools: Healthy Schools*, Sage, London, 1991.

HSE *Managing Occupational Stress: a Guide for Managers and Teachers in the Schools' Sector*, HMSO, London, 1990.

Kelly, M.J. *The Manchester Survey of Occupational Stress in Head-teachers and Principals in the United Kingdom*, Manchester Polytechnic, 1988.

Kemp, R. and Nathan, M. *Middle Management in Schools: a survival guide*, Blackwell, Oxford, 1989.

Madders, J. *Stress and Relaxation*, Macdonald and Co., London, 1979.

McKenzie, R.A. *The Time Trap*, AMACOM, New York, 1970.

NUT *Health and Safety. Teachers, Stress and Schools*, NUT, London, 1990.

Nelson-Jones, R. *Practical Counselling and Help Skills*, Cassell, London, 1992.

Nattras, S. 'Beating Stress', in *Teacher's Weekly* No. 138, 31 Jan. 1991, p7.

OU and Health Promotion Unit for Wales and the Health Education Authority, *Handling Stress*, Takeaway Taster, 1992.

Parkinson, M. 'Training the Counsellors – Stress Management', *Education and Training*, September 1985, p226.

Pease, A. *Body Language*, Sheldon Press, London, 1981.

Pearson, V. *Women and Power: Gaining Back Control*, Pavic Publications, Sheffield City Polytechnic, 1991.

Rees, F. *Teacher Stress: An Exploratory Study*, NFER, NAS/UWT, 1989.

Richards, J. H. 'Time Management – a review', *Work and Stress*, Vol. I. No. 1, 1987, pp.73–78.

Selye, H. *The Stress of Life*, McGraw-Hill, New York, 1956.

Selye, H. *The Stress of Life*, McGraw-Hill, New York, 1975.

Smythe, E. E. M. *Surviving Nursing*, Addison Wesley, London, pp 141-142, 1987.

Toffler, A. *Future Shock*, Bodley Head, New York, 1971.

Torrington, D. and Weightman, J. *The Reality of School Management*, Blackwell, Oxford, 1989.

Townend, A. *Assertion Training*, FPA Education Unit, London, 1985.

Index